UNIQUELY IMPERFECT, UNIQUELY QUALIFIED

OVERCOME ADVERSITY,
ESCAPE THE IMPERFECTION MENTALITY,
AND JOURNEY FROM SELF TO SERVE

UNIQUELY IMPERFECT, UNIQUELY QUALIFIED

OVERCOME ADVERSITY, ESCAPE THE IMPERFECTION MENTALITY, AND JOURNEY FROM SELF TO SERVE

DIANA LIGGITT FRITZ

UNIQUELY IMPERFECT, UNIQUELY QUALIFIED © 2025
by Diana Liggitt Fritz. All rights reserved.

Printed in the United States of America

Published by Igniting Souls
PO Box 43, Powell, OH 43065
IgnitingSouls.com

This book contains material protected under international and federal copyright laws and treaties. Any unauthorized reprint or use of this material is prohibited. No part of this book may be reproduced or transmitted in any form or by any means, electronic or mechanical, including photocopying, recording, or by any information storage and retrieval system, without express written permission from the author.

LCCN: 2024924418
Paperback ISBN: 978-1-63680-430-9
Hardcover ISBN: 978-1-63680-431-6
e-book ISBN: 978-1-63680-432-3

Available in paperback, hardcover, and e-book.

All Scripture quotations, unless otherwise indicated, are taken from the Holy Bible, New International Version®, NIV®. Copyright © 1973, 1978, 1984, 2011 by Biblica, Inc.™ Used by permission of Zondervan. All rights reserved worldwide. www.zondervan.com The "NIV" and "New International Version" are trademarks registered in the United States Patent and Trademark Office by Biblica, Inc.™

Any Internet addresses (websites, blogs, etc.) and telephone numbers printed in this book are offered as a resource. They are not intended in any way to be or imply an endorsement by Igniting Souls, nor does Igniting Souls vouch for the content of these sites and numbers for the life of this book.

Some names and identifying details may have been changed to protect the privacy of individuals.

Dedication

This book is dedicated to those who have walked with me, encouraged me, and laughed with me along this journey.

My sons Greyson and Benjamin who have hopefully watched an example of a positive mindset walking through the cancer storm.

My husband Bromley who has walked beside me into many difficult situations and supported me.

My parents who have stopped in to help whenever they could, and I can't imagine how hard it is to watch your child walk through the cancer journey.

My siblings, who encouraged, prayed, and supported me from afar, as well as hosted my boys multiple times during this journey.

My dear soul sister Kristine, who sacrificed many days/nights to travel with me to Miami, Texas, and wherever to fight this battle. She brought the fun to the journey.

To dear Dr. Kushner, who first diagnosed the cancer in 2014 and has not left my side. Every doctor needs to aspire to his level of true care and concern.

To Dr. David Tse, the first doctor I met at Bascom Palmer in 2014, who has continued to oversee, inspire, and ensure that all options are pursued—a true High Road Leader in his space.

Many friends and family (I can't name them all) who stepped in, brought a smile, sent a card, gave a hug, and checked on my family.

Each moment, each text, each card, each hug—all matter to help fight the battle.

Contents

Foreword ix
Introduction. xi
   Reflections from Those on the Journey xiii

PART I: Shaping Moments on the Journey

Chapter One: Grandma's Lessons Last a Lifetime 3
Chapter Two: Team Sports and Mental Resilience 11
Chapter Three: My First Knock Your
   Socks Off Moment 16
Chapter Four: Independence and Control. 25

PART II: My Cancer Journey

Chapter Five: Be Still… Please Come Into the Office. . . 37
Chapter Six: Is It in My Brain? 42
Chapter Seven: Joy Along the Journey 49
Chapter Eight: Back to Normal 59
Chapter Nine: More Lessons on the Journey 67
Chapter Ten: The End of the Year of 40…
   Missed the Mark. 74

Chapter Eleven: Single Mom with So Much to Balance . . 80
Chapter Twelve: Five Years Cancer Free… Almost 85
Chapter Thirteen: Back Again 97
Chapter Fourteen: New Normal and New Changes . . . 106

PART III: Uniquely Imperfect

Chapter Fifteen: New Year, New Challenges 133
Chapter Sixteen: Back Home, New Look 152
Chapter Seventeen: Seven Weeks Away from Home . . 162
Chapter Eighteen: Why Not Now?
    This Unique Look Makes Me Memorable 175
Chapter Nineteen: What Is Normal? 192
Chapter Twenty: The Journey Continues 198
Afterword 215
Acknowledgments 219
About the Author 221

Foreword

The first time Diana Fritz told me about the book you're holding, I knew it would make an impact. Diana shares her journey with a spirit so full of hope and anticipation that I was certain her story would connect with hearts and lives in a truly meaningful way. This is more than a story about facing cancer—it's a story about faith, courage, and choosing to live with purpose even when life takes unexpected turns.

In 2024, it was estimated that over two million people would receive a cancer diagnosis. These are real lives—people we know and care about. Yet, what Diana has shown us is that a diagnosis, while difficult, doesn't have to be the defining chapter of someone's story. Cancer can introduce new perspectives, create deeper relationships, and, as Diana demonstrates so well, even open doors to a new purpose.

As the CEO of Maxwell Leadership, I've seen Diana show up time and again with a spirit of service that inspires everyone she encounters. At our events, she's been a greeter, an usher, and a friendly face in the Gear Store, bringing encouragement wherever she goes. Diana embodies resilience. She doesn't just press forward in her own journey; she lifts others as she goes, always choosing to serve and uplift.

In this book, you will discover that life's struggles can be lightened with laughter and that choosing positivity—even when it's hard—is a powerful act of strength. Diana's journey is a testament to this, and it's a privilege to be a part of sharing her story.

In *Uniquely Imperfect, Uniquely Qualified*, Diana invites you to walk with her through the highs and lows of her journey. If you're dealing with a recent cancer diagnosis, you'll find Diana's honesty and transparency a source of hope and inspiration. Her story isn't just about survival; it's about discovering strength in unexpected places, choosing faith over fear, and continuing forward with grace.

At the end of each chapter, Diana provides reflections and application questions, inviting you to reflect on your own journey. I encourage you to engage with these moments of self-reflection; they're more than just words—they're an invitation to grow.

Diana's story reminds us that no matter the challenges we face, we each have the capacity to add value, to bring hope, and to be a light in the lives of others. In this journey with Diana, may you find your own strength, purpose, and resilience.

Mark Cole
CEO Maxwell Leadership Enterprises

Introduction

I had just turned forty when I got the news. "That spot near your eye that's been bothering you is a rare form of cancer." In that moment, I couldn't help but think, *Why me? Why now?* I was a single mom with two young boys at home, counting on me. *How would this affect them? How would we get through it?*

Fortunately, God sent an angel to remind me of the lessons I'd learned and help shift my thinking. My prayer changed. *Okay, God, who do you need me to be a light to?*

Though it may have been the biggest hurdle, cancer wasn't the first hardship I faced in my life. I had endured sports injuries and divorce. In fact, many events in my past have become pivotal moments. Playing team sports, learning from my grandmother, and executive lessons all connected me to a quote from Victor Frankl, "Everything can be taken from a man but one thing: the last of the human freedoms—to choose one's attitude in any given set of circumstances, to choose one's own way." Many years before my diagnosis, I decided no one could steal my power to choose my response.

Today, more than two million people are diagnosed with cancer every year.[1] But unfortunately, the *why me* attitude I had initially isn't limited to those who have received a scary

---

[1] *American Cancer Society. Cancer Facts & Figures 2024.* Atlanta: American Cancer Society; 2024.

Introduction

prognosis. Many Americans struggle with negativity. Because they focus on their imperfections, they get stuck. Their attitude becomes as debilitating as a potentially terminal illness.

Attitude is everything when you're fighting cancer. We have to first adopt the mindset that the journey isn't over. My new look is a bit unique and memorable, and I'm hoping this book will be as well. I want each page to spark memories and let you pause for reflection. My goal is to help others move past their "cancers" and adversity so they can serve and shine.

One Eye.
One Life.
One Day.
One Hour.
One Second.
Each One Matters.

Every day, I ask myself, "Did I live today like One Matters?" At some point, nearly everyone experiences a "Knock Your Socks Off" moment that forces us to make a choice. We can become bitter, or we can become better. If we choose bitter, will we miss moments that matter—moments that otherwise would not come our way? I strive daily to pick better and am beyond blessed by the unseen benefits along the way.

Friends, I pray you'll join me as I share my story. I hope each moment helps you find the light in your own journey. At the end of each chapter, you'll find reflection questions to reveal the power in your own story. Be prepared to smile, laugh, and cry.

I realize not everyone can relate to a cancer journey or the physical imperfections it caused me. At the same time, I think most of us understand what it's like to feel imperfect and inadequate. Cancers and adversities hit everyone along the way. But we can still thrive and add value to those around us.

My story is the testimony of one uniquely imperfect person who found ways to fulfill my purpose. As I shift away from a focus on why me, I have touching moments that allow me to serve and be a light.

I hope my story helps you see that though you feel Uniquely Imperfect, you, too, are Uniquely Qualified. Arise and shine because each One Matters.

REFLECTIONS FROM Those ON THE JOURNEY

"[This] story is a testament to human kindness, incredible resilience, and perseverance. [Diana's] battle with cancer is a shining example of [her] toughness, insight, and grace—qualities that define [her] in everything [she] does. [She] confronts cancer with dignity, determination, and an unwavering will to fight. [Diana] is an exemplar of courage. Cancer handed [her] a pair of red-hot shoes and forced [her] to dance with uncertainty every day for the rest of [her] life.

[Diana's] willingness to be open and transparent about [her] diagnosis provides a breathtaking window into [her] character. And while cancer was terrible, [she] continued to find hope, which [she] shared through many heartbreaking and honest emails and public speaking engagements laced with contagious gratitude.

I deeply respect and admire [Diana] for [her] unwavering positivity—[she] never complains or shows bitterness in confronting adversity. [She] uplifts the spirits of people around [her]. [Her] authentic, unfakeable smiles make people feel at ease."

David T. Tse, M.D., F.A.C.S.
Bascom Palmer Eye Institute||University of Miami Health Systems
Vice-Chair of Administration and Strategic Planning
Professor of Ophthalmology, Dermatology, Otolaryngology, and Neurosurgery

Introduction

"I have been following Diana, suffering from a rare type of cancer, for 12 or 13 years now through incredible trials of multiple facial and ocular surgeries, chemotherapy, immunotherapy, intra-arterial chemo, radiation, and gamma knife surgery. This has required extensive travel and time away from her home and her children. Through it all, she has continued to work, raise two boys, provide for her family, and evince a positive attitude of courage, resilience, and remarkably good humor. She has shown patience and understanding and has been inspirational to her friends, her family, her coworkers, her doctors, and providers. In my 58 years of medical practice, no patient in my memory has shown the limits of endurance, faith, tenacity, and courage that has motivated all of us in the shadow of her journey."

Hal Kushner MD FACS
Col. US Army (Ret.)

"Diana is the true hero in the room. What she has undergone is not easy, and she is still smiling and caring for her two boys. Boys: Your mom is the hero in the room."

Duane Dieter
Founder and Developer of Close Quarters Defense

PART I
Shaping Moments on the Journey

Success or failure doesn't happen by accident or coincidence. Every moment of our journey is shaped by our intentions. Many ask about the source of my joy and tell me my attitude encourages them. "How can you smile in the middle of adversity?"

These compliments lead me to reflect on the pivotal moments of my life and the people who brought me through my formative years. I appreciate each person and event that helped me develop my current mindset and approach to life, laying the foundation for joy as I walked through my cancer journey.

CHAPTER ONE

Grandma's Lessons Last a Lifetime

My grandmother gave me my first view of Jesus here on Earth. The spiritual rock for the Liggitt family, Gram demonstrated peace and calm no matter what her family endured. Her laugh, smile, and mandatory hugs reflected the love and grace that poured out from her.

I recall many conversations around the kitchen table where she would lift a caring inquiry about a person she knew was struggling. She found the good in everyone without difficulty. Regardless of the circumstances, she saw some glimmer of hope in every person. People were not always faithful to her, yet she was always faithful to them. I'm confident Gram spent many a morning before the sun rose in her prayer chair and on her knees talking to Jesus and giving Him her hurts and cares. Not only did she shine, she also provided and fought for grace for those who had fallen away.

Grandma's Lessons Last a Lifetime

Each summer, my sister, brother, and I spent a full week at Gram and Pap's. We looked forward to the hugs, laughs, and home-cooked food. Each morning, a kitchen full of light and warm hugs greeted us before we sat down around the long kitchen table for breakfast. Gram started the meal with prayer and ended with a devotional from a little red book about the size of an index card or a scripture reading from the old army green Bible.

Our outdoor chores followed breakfast. And though I'm sure I would have complained about working outside first thing in the morning at home, there was something different about the assignment at Gram's house. We painted old wagon wheels for decoration, picked up sticks across the multi-acre property, and cleaned the basement. Whatever Gram asked us to do, we willingly did. After we finished, afternoons or early evenings promised treats that ranged from ice cream and mini-golfing at Blue Lantern to swimming at Beltsville.

Going to church was an expected part of visiting my grandparents. We always arrived early for Sunday School, and each time, she would lead us to our class as though it was our first visit. She taught the college-aged class, and I was blessed to have her as a teacher for a few summers.

She had a gift for connecting people with her warm smile. If I couldn't find her, I simply had to listen for her laugh. Of course, I could also ask anyone in the building if they had seen Jean. I always thought Gram was something of a celebrity at church, which made me hold her in even higher esteem at home. Everyone knew her and felt blessed to see her.

Gram painted a vivid picture of Jesus for me in so many areas of her life. She wrote letters to those in prison and the military. I'm not sure they could read her broad cursive letters, but without a doubt, they knew she cared and prayed for them. When I shifted to my college days, I received some of those letters filled with what she and Pap had been up to. She ended each one with her encouraging words—"Stay Close to Jesus." Often, she included a few dollars and suggested I take a friend out for ice cream.

During my freshman year in college, I was required to write about a person who had influenced my life. I considered writing about my parents or my high school basketball coach. They made indelible impacts on my life. However, I chose Gram. She gave me my view of Jesus on Earth. Through the years, I watched her love and find goodness in the fallen sinner, keep in touch with the ex-girlfriend who was discarded by everyone else, and defend even the most hopeless.

Gram called me "the supervisor." At large family meals, often Sunday after church and holidays, I made my mark by giving directions and escaping to the bathroom while the adults assigned dishwashing duties. She also called me "snoopy." When something was lost or hidden, I had a gift for finding it.

My grandmother lived a life of sacrifice and service. Her nursing education ended before it could get started because she found herself pregnant and married at fifteen. She was so proud of me for finishing college and being her first grandchild to receive a Master's degree. In one season of her life, she cared for her mother and mentally retarded brother, yet still found time to serve at church or take meals and desserts to those that were homebound.

She showed love to everyone. Still, she kept her guard up when it came to certain topics or people. When the Jehovah's Witness team showed up, she would converse with them for an hour on the front porch, but they were never invited into the house. I'm not sure why; I never asked.

Anyone else received a hug and a warm welcome. It was not optional. She loved greeting people and bringing them into her humble farmhouse. I don't think anyone noticed her aging furniture and decor or that the big brown farmhouse table always wobbled. When love takes over, people forget about the flaws and enjoy being in your presence.

Gram had a way of connecting fun phrases or comments that helped me learn to reflect rather than defend. And when she stayed with us, the grandchild who gave up their room for her and Pap often found money under the mattress to thank them for sharing their space.

Memories in Abundance

I clearly remember that evening in January when my former husband met me at the end of the driveway to let me know Gram had passed and gone to meet Jesus. As a young executive, I had a list of work to do, but that was all forgotten quickly.

My mother had called days earlier to let me know the end was near. And I had debated and prayed about flying from Florida to Pennsylvania to visit her in the hospital one last time. I elected to cherish my last vivid memories of our last Christmas dinner together instead. Our family of twenty-five-plus sat at a long table for dinner, and I took the seat beside her. Through her smiles and laughter, I saw her struggling to breathe more than in prior years. That was the memory and visual I wanted to keep with me.

At her funeral, many told me, "You have her smile." I can still picture standing at the back of the church, touching her hand with tears in my eyes as one kind person tapped on my shoulder to compliment me. Her encouragement caught me off guard and filled me with emotion. Each person's words were so sincere. "To have her smile" was an honor and a challenge. I want to always carry her smile forward.

My public speaking skills were in their refinement stage when I volunteered to speak at her funeral on behalf of the Liggitt grandchildren. Yet, I knew that she deserved to be honored, and she saw no fear that blocked her from following her God. So, I offered to share, and I am so blessed that I did.

This is an excerpt of what I shared that day:

> When I was a freshman in college, I had to write a story about my hero (it could not be Jesus). My immediate thought was to write about her. She was so much like Jesus—loving, caring, giving, a prayer warrior, and always looking for the best in others. She loved people. She would take us with her to deliver meals to a shut-in or baked goods to a new neighbor. She invited everyone to church. She cared for her mom and brother until they passed away; it might have been easier to allow someone else to do it; she sacrificed so much to care for them. That leaves a lasting impression on all of us.
>
> When her health started to deteriorate, she never lost her faith. Whenever I talked with her on the

phone or visited, she would tell me how good God was. She never lost that smile. It was a reflection of all God's goodness inside of her.

Now, she is smiling more than ever, and we will always remember her glow. Her example has inspired us all, and our greatest compliment to her is to do our best to live out the traits she so beautifully exemplified for us. I'd like to close our thoughts today with some of her closing statements in our letters or on the phone:

> Same Here
> *You are loved and appreciated by Jesus and us.*
> Seek God's best in all you do
> Keep Close to Jesus

Plus, we shared the song that the cousins performed to the tune of "The Land of Hatchy Milatchy" at my grandparents' 50th Anniversary:

There's cookies and spice cake and 10:00 news
    In the land of Pappy and Grammy
There's cashews and candy and swimming at Beltsville
    In the land of Pappy and Grammy.
There's trips to Blue Lantern and lots of old pictures
    On the living room wall
There's pickup sticks, steak sandwiches, and
    Pierogies, Klindikes, and ice pops for all
There's a big old green Bible and a little red book
    In the land of Pappy and Grammy
There's trips to Lake Dorie and Gananoque
    In the land of Pappy and Grammy
There's big Sunday dinners and holiday pies
    And macaroni & cheese

Uniquely Imperfect, Uniquely Qualified

> The old hunting cabin in Sullivan County
>   And rope swings hanging from trees
> There's big hugs and kisses and lots of love shown
>   In the land of Pappy and Grammy

If I had an endless supply of money, Gram's farm would still be the haven she provided for so many. I wanted to buy the old house. I cherish the memories we created there and the reminders it brings of what it means to shine and be a light.

I have so many stories of laughter and silly moments with Gram—memories of her sacrifice and how she connected with me and filled me with belief. My grandmother always saw me as a ten, just like Jesus sees me. She shaped the person I am today and influenced my response to adversity. She demonstrated grace under fire.

Over the past ten years, many have commented about my poise and peace during this trying season, and I think back to Gram. As I reflect on the ups and downs of my life, her example of unconditional love and grace rings strong in my heart. Her life shaped my character and my view of a relationship with God. She had a heart for God's people and refused to create boundaries to their possibilities.

Recently, a family member reached out to let me know I reminded her of my dear Grandmother. Her comments caused me to pause and sit with my tears for a moment. I miss her. She never got to meet my boys. Is she looking over me with pride as I navigate this journey of life?

"Gram, I try to love like you did and show grace under fire. Thank you for your influence on my life. I pray it shines through to others."

Reflection

As I reflect on Gram's impact, I feel exceedingly blessed. I also wish I could travel back in time and relive some of those moments. Losing people we love is a reality of life, yet I strive to reflect on what I admire most about those precious souls and then carry that quality forward. As I facilitate DISC® Communication Workshops, I start each session by reminding the group how their personalities and communication styles were shaped—heredity, environment, and role models. When I ask which role models shaped them most, mom or grandma is nearly always mentioned.

- Who was that "Gram" in your life?
- When dear loved ones pass, we mourn. But we should also reflect on how we can honor them based on what they taught us. How can you continue their legacy? What are you doing to continue the legacy of those that have most impacted your life?
- What are some of the greatest memories from that person? Are you passing those concepts on to the next generation?

Application

- Pause – take time to believe in someone near you who doesn't see worth in themselves. That person may be you. You matter, and One Matters.
- Listen for the nudge to brighten someone's day. Simple is still life-changing. Don't overthink or complicate.

CHAPTER TWO

Team Sports and Mental Resilience

In my small, private Christian elementary school, I didn't have the opportunity to play sports. Because the school leveraged the A.C.E. (Accelerated Christian Education) program, I spent each school day in a cubicle working through lessons independently. Though I could move through the subjects at my own PACE, the individual study made lunchtime ping pong the most engaging part of my day.

Middle school changed everything. Our family transitioned to a more traditional Christian school with teachers and classrooms when I hit sixth grade. And the following year, I discovered basketball. Jack Fox started as a traditional coach but grew to be a second father figure to me.

The lessons his coaching and leadership taught shaped me more than I recognized in the moment. I learned the discipline of following team rules. For instance, one did not miss practice without a solid excuse. Regardless of your skill, you lost playing time for your absence.

He encouraged us to "talk with each other" rather than go to the coach to complain or show frustration. We took turns sharing a devotion at practice giving us early public speaking skills. Team captains interacted with teammates directly on challenges instead of complaining to the coach.

Coach also brought us experiences outside of basketball. We volunteered, spent time building relationships with parties at his house, watched college basketball together, attended camps, and learned about successful players and disciplines.

Because my elementary program allowed me to move ahead as quickly as I could, I ended up being a year or two ahead of others my age. Being so much younger meant I was often pushed outside my comfort zone at basketball camp. I felt overwhelmed and intimidated the first time I attended a summer basketball camp at a local high school. They had more than just a school; it was an entire campus. Coach Fox stopped by every afternoon to see how his team was doing. He never left without giving us pointers to use the next day.

On the sidelines during a game, Coach Fox got serious; however, he was famous for weaving humor into practice and other activities. One evening, he took my sister and me to a local semi-pro baseball game. The bat boy intrigued him, and he found a way to catch his eye and hint that I had a crush on him. I never lived down Coach's joke. Stories like that often found their way into tense moments to spark laughter and lighten the situation.

A natural team player, I didn't focus on my points or statistics; I wanted the team to win. Maybe a team mentality comes more naturally to a middle child. I simply know the individual stats didn't drive me. For example, I was determined to graduate from high school a year early to head to college. Coach wanted me to stay one more year so I could break the 1,000-point or rebound milestones. But those weren't important to me. I felt honored to have my name in the paper on occasion, but getting a signed basketball for personal achievement just didn't motivate me. I loved making an impact on the team, but personal accolades weren't enough for me to stay in high school for an extra year.

The mental tenacity and endurance our coach challenged us to grow have been instrumental in helping me develop a uniquely imperfect, uniquely qualified mindset. He taught us mental tenacity or how to be mentally tough. This meant I learned not to give in when I was tired, someone scored on me, or I got blocked. It was a mindset shift and a commitment to keep fighting until the end. It is a game-changer in sports.

If I hang my head when I miss a shot, I likely will be scored on the next run down the court. Mentally tough players just keep playing. It's the self-talk difference: "Okay, I missed. The game isn't over. Just get the ball back." versus "That's the second shot I've missed. Hope coach doesn't pull me out."

I remember those antagonistic teams with members who were poor sports. While others let their taunts and attitudes bother them, I just kept playing, ignoring the strain and tension they caused. Some of my teammates had a hard time celebrating our victories because they focused on the frustration of their personal stats. I always had a hard time understanding that. We won—wasn't that the goal? The game wasn't about me and my stats. Basketball is a team sport. If we all worked together for the win, isn't that what mattered?

In one of our Regional Playoffs, I was assigned to guard the best player on the other team. Because I kept her scoring in the single digits, they gave me the Tournament MVP award. I didn't score the most points. Many who didn't know basketball well might not have even paid attention to my position. That recognition for providing a solid defense still means a lot to me. It wasn't about the scoring charts, my victory was playing a key role in the team's success.

That life lesson has stuck with me more than many others, and I strive to share it with youth who think they need to see their name on the charts or be the hero. Many miss the reward that comes from making a difference where they are most gifted, not necessarily the most decorated. Focusing on what we contribute instead of recognition and fame often brings unexpected recognition. Don't try to be someone you don't resonate with. Team sports helped me develop an important mindset: Life is not about you.

I reached out to Coach Fox a few years back to thank him for his lessons. It became evident to me many adults have never played team sports or had a coach who instilled the meaning of team. I watch individuals with virtual blinders focus on themselves and neglect their impact on the company and the rest of the team.

When I consult, I observe employees tattling to their manager instead of having those conversations that build relationships and create strong teams. I use those opportunities to share those great team lessons from Coach Fox as well as team videos to remind them how the workplace can be an encouraging, cooperative team experience.

It's that same mental resilience and team spirit that helped me through my bouts with cancer. Working together with a positive mindset makes all the difference.

Reflection

As I reflect on Coach Fox and the impact of team sports on my life, I am incredibly thankful for the investment he made in me. I learned how to be a humble, hard-working, committed, and accountable team player, as well as how to be mentally tough on and off the court. I watch many coaches and cringe; youth sports should not be about getting a player to the pros. When we focus exclusively on the material outcome, we miss the opportunity to teach teamwork, accountability, leadership, and mental tenacity—key lessons for life.

- Who was that "Coach" that pushed you to stretch and grow?
- How is your mental tenacity? Do you react impulsively to situations causing tension and strife, or do you have conversations, keeping your mind focused on positivity so you can stay strong?

Application

- Pause – What is your current mental tenacity level? Are you giving in when an obstacle hits (i.e., someone blocks your shot)? What is your source of strength and peace?
- Are you motivated more by personal accolades, attention, or the greater purpose or team?
- When you lose a "game," do you learn and keep moving or allow your personal "stats" to steal your concentration?

CHAPTER THREE

My First Knock Your Socks Off Moment

Despite suggestions to stay back a year, I had my sights set on graduating at sixteen and attending Messiah College shortly after my next birthday. In my very independent and silently rebellious mind, it seemed logical to graduate early and play college basketball.

On October 21, 1991, after breakfast in the college cafeteria, I checked the posted roster. Just a couple of months after my first day of college, I discovered I reached my goal. I made the basketball team. Practice started immediately, and two days later, while challenging myself during a drill, I pushed too far. I threw the ball forward, then raced to grab it and make the shot to score before I went out of bounds. I can still hear the "pop" as I landed awkwardly after the lay-up. My leg wouldn't hold me. I knew something had gone wrong.

A few days later, I learned the full impact of my injury. My first "Knock Your Socks Off" moment came in the form of a season-ending torn ACL in my right knee. Navigating the medical world was uncharted waters for me. In high school, chiropractor visits were my biggest exposure to doctors. But I faced it head-on as I maneuvered through x-rays, an MRI, arthroscopic surgery, and finally, ACL reconstruction the week before Christmas.

A simple prayer I wrote in my journal at the end of that year reflected my growing maturity:

> *Right now, God, I'm very glad you led me to college. I enjoyed my first year, and I met many new people. Thanks for helping me make the basketball team. God, I don't know why you allowed me to get hurt, but I believe there is a lesson for me to be learned. Please help me to learn it and accept what you are trying to show me.*

My reason for going to college at sixteen quickly faded. Thankfully, at the time, I was reading Victor Frankl's *A Man's Search for Meaning*. This was truly God's timing. The book starts out a little dry, particularly for a young college freshman. Yet, I grasped the point and the application and realized my plight was nothing. Tortured, beaten, and starved in a Nazi prison camp, Frankl still had free will to choose his response; he was not a victim. As Stephen Covey states in *The 7 Habits of Highly Effective People*, our language can indicate whether our thoughts are primarily proactive or reactive. Reactive words and self-talk include words and thoughts like "I can't do this," "It's all over," and "I give up." Proactive thoughts and words may require a pause and then,

"Okay, let's move forward," "There is still a way," and "What is the positive in this?"

If Victor Frankl could choose to be positive and proactive toward the prison guards who starved and beat him, then certainly I could find something positive in my journey. Mental tenacity helped me shift the focus from the negativity of the things I don't get to do and what I am required to do to everything I get to do and who I am able to meet.

About that time, I wrote a few paragraphs in English literature about cancer. When I happened across it not long ago in a bag of random papers in my closet, it brought chills. When I wrote my thoughts at age seventeen, I never dreamt I would someday live out my message.

Uniquely Imperfect, Uniquely Qualified

Diana Liggitt

A 15

If a person learns that they have cancer or another disease that can take their life. They will feel trapped and will realize that life is not fair. They will ask God why he allowed them to get a disease, what did they do wrong. This is disease that they must have tremendous faith in God. In the midst of trying times, they must know by faith that God holds the future in His hands. Faith is the first key to free ourselves from depression.

They must then accept the disease. No one goes through life without some difficulties. Faith will allow you to accept your circumstances. *a key — see it from God's point of view.*

Then we are free to choose our response. A person can allow the disease to control their actions, but they can also make the most of their lives.

We are free to act when we wait on the Lord for direction they can help others in the situation that they are in, or we can pity ourselves.

After one was done all the other steps they are free to love. A person that has a disease may be ridiculed by others. They are free to love them no matter what they have done.

The best way to solve a problem is to say yes and accept the circumstances. — 1 Thess. 5:18

> If a person learns that they have cancer or another disease that can take their life, they will feel trapped and will realize that life is not fair. They will ask God why he allowed them to get a disease, what did they do wrong.
>
> This is disease that they must have tremendous faith in God. In the midst of trying times, they must know by faith that God holds the future in His hands. Faith is the first key to free ourselves from depression.
>
> They must then accept the disease. No one goes through life without some difficulties. Faith will allow you to accept your circumstances.
>
> Then we are free to choose our response. A person can allow the disease to control their actions, but they can also make the most of their lives.
>
> We are free to act when we wait on the Lord for direction. They can help others in the situation that they are in, or we can pity ourselves.
>
> After one was done all other steps, they are free to love. A person that has a disease may be ridiculed by others. They are free to love them no matter what they have done.
>
> The best way to solve a problem is to say yes and accept the circumstances.

I quickly recovered from my knee surgery, and the doctor cleared me to play again in my sophomore year after eight and a half months. In retrospect, I realize I gave my training and strength exercises about ninety percent. Coach gave me the option of taking a second season off to build more strength. But I really wanted to go with the team to the

Bahamas over Christmas, so I pushed ahead. I didn't pause to check with God; I just kept moving forward.

About three days before my annual check-up for my ACL surgery, I landed on a teammate's shoe during a drill and twisted my knee. "Pop!" I heard that familiar sound again. But this time, I had a brace on, so even though I felt a bit off, I just kept going. The coaches needed someone to finish the drills for the day. Training room visits had become all too familiar for me, and before I headed home, I stopped to get some ice.

When I walked into the surgeon's office for that annual follow-up, I knew my ACL was torn again. Most post-recovery athletes tear the opposite ACL because they favor the injured knee. Not me, I re-injured my right ACL. The doctor provided two options for this second surgery. I could use the patella tendon from my left knee—I had used the right one the first time—or he could use a cadaver Achilles tendon.

At the time, a cadaver seemed risky. Magic Johnson had just announced his premature retirement from basketball the year before, and Johnson's wasn't the only AIDS story that stirred our fear. My parents and I asked many questions to confirm the cadaver was disease-free before agreeing to that option.

My First Knock Your Socks Off Moment

I might as well have stayed the extra year in high school. My motive for going early faded overnight. The day before my January surgery, I wrote my prayer:

Dear God, my loving Father,

Well, tomorrow I go in for surgery for the fourth time for the same knee. People ask me if I'm nervous or scared. I am neither. It's hard to describe how I feel. I seem to have a calm assurance and believe that You are taking care of me. I don't need to worry about tomorrow cuz you're already there. God, maybe you didn't want me to play basketball again, and I'm sorry for leaving your side. God, thank you for my doctor, and please work through him to repair my knee.

Recovery was different and quicker using the cadaver's ACL rather than my own. My minutes of playing were very limited my sophomore year in college. Still, I strove to be a solid teammate and encourager on the bench. And on a positive note, I made it to the Bahamas and enjoyed the time with the team.

I am not sure the Bahamas trip was worth a second ACL surgery. Yet, in retrospect, I realize this adversity opened doors for mentors, coaches, and friends I otherwise would not have. Prior to this injury, my major was "undecided." But rehab in the training room allowed me to get to know the Head Athletic Trainer and Men's Basketball Coach. They inspired me to shift my degree to Exercise Science and find internships with Sports Information. A new career vision came from the injury. Though I've switched careers since then, the lessons I learned and my mentors' impact provided valuable life lessons. Without the injury, I would not have connected with the next step in my journey—Sports Information Director at Palm Beach Atlantic combined with working on my MBA.

Reflection

As I reflect on my first "Knock Your Socks Off" moment, I am incredibly thankful for the timing of mentors and Victor Frank's book assignment in English literature. Learning the meaning of the word "proactive" and the power of a positive mindset provided pivotal lessons at a critical time in my life. Take a minute to reflect:

My First Knock Your Socks Off Moment

- Name some "Knock Your Socks Off" moments in your earlier life. Did you learn from those situations and move on, or are you still stuck in those moments?
- What people kept you moving forward?

Application

- Pause – Stop and thank those friends and family members who mentored and guided you forward in that season.
- Who do you know who is struggling right now with a setback? Look and listen for the timing to encourage and mentor them on the opportunity in the pain.

CHAPTER FOUR

Independence and Control

As I look back on younger me, I realize I didn't like the unknown. It was uncomfortable, and I hadn't learned to pause and ask for directions. By the time I finished my Master's degree, I had many questions about my future, but because I'd let God get distant, I didn't think to consult Him. *What's next? Where will I live? What job should I apply for?*

When my boyfriend proposed, I saw that as an answer to one of life's tough questions. Saying yes closed the door on a couple of unknowns. Despite the red flags and warnings from family and friends, I said yes, and we married. The first few years were pleasant and engaging. We bought our first house, grew in our careers, and learned to be a married couple.

The earliest indicators of problems came when I started to outpace him in our career growth. And when we decided to start a family, the chasm widened. Despite multiple attempts and fertility treatments, children weren't in our future. Within a few months, the distance grew unmanageable. We

Independence and Control

were just two people living in the same house. After an amicable divorce, we both set out on new journeys.

Without acknowledging my wounded heart, I started to date and explore dating sites. I met some interesting men and ended up with many fun stories to tell. But without guidance from God, my middle-child mentality went into rescue mode. I failed to exercise caution and didn't think about looking for a balanced relationship. Instead, I took on the role of fixer, making sure everything was going well for the men I met and dated.

In less than a year, I had met someone, and the couple commitments expanded, yet the relationship and balance as partner and true friends were not strong. It's hard to recognize in the middle of the chaos. Many of my friends and family suggested it was too soon for dating, let alone a wedding. Others warned this wasn't the right relationship. Yet, I was still determined to move forward with a wedding; I was not ready or willing to listen to the voices outside my head. I'm sure when they came out to show their support on our wedding day, they had serious doubts about my choices. Yet, many came to show support at our sunrise wedding on the beach.

Even though I finally was able to have a family, within three years, our relationship and the home dynamic were far from healthy. By the time my second son was born, I had a decision to make. Would I hold true to my marriage covenant or provide a safe space for my boys?

For the first time in my life, I prayed and truly listened and waited for God to speak. I journaled and listened to pastors and friends. I learned to reframe questions so I could get to the heart of what people really thought.

One night, as I sat in my recliner with my four-year-old sleeping on my lap, I heard the words "Go Now." The sun was just barely over the horizon when I left with my children and never looked back.

The boys and I moved into a condo to start a new life. I didn't comprehend how the changes and the uncertainty that came with them would affect an eighteen-month-old and a four-year-old. Greyson, my oldest, struggled but had no idea how to articulate his confusion. It affected his behavior, and I had no idea how to interpret or help with the outbursts.

I started reading parenting books and endured moments of embarrassment at restaurants, stores, and schools as my little one struggled to understand what was going on in his life. It broke my heart to see this smart little boy wrestle with life.

Despite two failed marriages, I still felt blessed with my career and my friends' support. But I knew I needed more. I went to a few counselors to get help for my boys. One counselor rocked my world at our very first session. He listened to the stories of the challenges I was having with my son.

As we wrapped up, I asked, "When can you meet my son?"

His reply stopped me short. "What if the only person that needs to change is you?"

Wait. What? I did not make that appointment to fix myself. My son needed help.

That became a powerful and pivotal question of reflection as I worked to improve as a parent. I wish I could say that the magic question made parenting easy. But it took months and years, as well as many people pouring into my kids, to get us through that time. I am blessed with the young men they are today.

Being a parent was and is one of the most humbling experiences of life. I often presented before crowds of three hundred for my job. These men and women listened, interacted, and followed directions. Never mind that an hour earlier, I was

Independence and Control

pulling a fighting toddler out of the car seat to get him into the preschool or trying to get him to stop hitting me.

During those years, I learned I don't know all the answers. Not only is it okay to pause and wait on God for direction, but it's also imperative. I don't need to know what's happening tomorrow. I need to trust God for guidance. Before I took the boys and left, I had been praying for direction for months. Many had shared their opinions of what I should do when, but no one was in my shoes in my situation. No one saw what I saw or experienced what I experienced. Thus, those subtle words "Go Now" were critical. They gave me direction as well as the power to act on them.

Very few knew that for about a month, I lived with my dear friend until I found the condo. I continued to be balanced and stoic in the professional environment, though inside, I was falling apart. I even addressed a crowd at the company kickoff with a joke about love and marriage. Only a few sensed I was distracted.

Though I'd grown up in the church, I spent many of my adult years just showing up on Sundays. I had never allowed the church to be the church, and I hadn't participated as part of the family. Don't get me wrong, showing up on Sundays with two young boys in tow was an accomplishment. Yet, God calls us His children and asks us to serve and be the church. He invites us to allow others to help us and share our burdens.

During this time of leaning on God, He helped me see how to be a part of the church as an adult, single mom, and young executive. I joined Wednesday night parenting classes, volunteered in children's church, and worked to be a part of the church versus an attendee of the church. I realized I didn't need to pretend to have it all together walking in the doors. It was okay to ask for help, prayer, and guidance.

I'm grateful for everything I learned from my failures. They taught me to walk in peace and in patience even though the road was rough and dark. I learned to wait in discomfort rather than rush into the first answer that seemed to alleviate the unknown—as a mom, these times taught me how to be creative and ask for help. I became an advocate for my son when a teacher wouldn't communicate with me. And perhaps most importantly, I discovered what it means to be a part of a church family, ask for guidance, and seek counsel from those who are wiser in their years.

Reflection

As I reflect on my old tendency of balancing control and pleasing others, I see the challenges it caused. It's okay to be uncomfortable, to not know what is next. Clarity for tomorrow is not guaranteed today. We must pause and wait for guidance. I continue to reflect on a few questions. Take a minute and write down your thoughts.

- In what areas of your life do you fight for control and feel the tension?
    - o
    - o
    - o

- In what areas do you attempt to fix the other person and possibly miss opportunities for self-awareness?
- In what areas have you asked God for guidance without waiting for a response?

Application

- Review the areas at the top of the list for "fighting for control." Practice writing those in your journal and "let them go" for a day or two. Then, come back and jot down the insight from the pause.
- Review the list of people you keep trying to fix and ask yourself why. Take time to respond to the question, "What if the only person I need to fix is me?" What can you change to avoid the tension?

PART II

My Cancer Journey

During that year, between thirty-nine and forty, I constantly moved between uncertainty and clarity. I faced divorce and being a single parent. Life felt like a balancing act.

In October 2013, I visited a Florida Health Urgent Care facility for a sinus infection. The kind doctor provided a plan for my sinuses, but "bumps" on the caruncle of my left eye troubled him. (Yes, you may need to Google that.) He suggested I visit an ophthalmologist. My mind resisted. *I'm a single mom, and I have to work. I don't have time.* Despite my brain's protests and a belief it was nothing, I scheduled the appointment.

I expected to be in and out in an hour or less when I walked into the ophthalmologist's office about a month later. The first doctor I met didn't recognize the symptoms. So she called in her colleague, Dr. Hal Kushner. He was an expert in the field. He took a look and prescribed steroid drops for six weeks. Before I left, a nurse took photos of my eye. If the cyst didn't get smaller, I would need surgery.

The six-week mark fell just before Christmas. I was certain the bump had shrunk, but the nurse's photo proved me wrong, so they scheduled an outpatient surgery for January. I have had multiple surgeries over the years—a knee, a C-section, wisdom teeth, etc.—but for some reason, I dreaded this same-day procedure on my eye.

My parents took the boys for New Year's Eve, so I enjoyed my solo celebration and took some time to be alone with God. I had gone to a Beth Moore conference just before the end of the year. That event challenged my ability and willingness to trust again. But my latest diagnosis was teaching me to trust on a whole new level.

As I reflected on the prior year and outlined some important milestones for 2014, I noted how much easier it is to have faith and trust for big things—things that are outside my realm of expertise. I had no control over my current circumstances. Yet somehow, it seemed more natural to trust God to bring me the right doctors, be in charge of my appointments, and take care of what I couldn't than to ask him to work in the day-to-day.

As I considered the list, I started thinking about what one thing on my bucket list I wanted to be sure to check off. With the many changes in my life over the last twelve months—becoming a single parent, living in a new place, the new opportunities with the boys, and my fortieth birthday getting closer each day—my list of goals for 2014 included a variety of new items.

- Try yoga. This was way outside my comfort zone.
- Go on a mission trip before 40.
- Stop seeing men as bad and assuming they have an ulterior motive.

- Let down my guard so I can trust people and allow others to help me.
- Help Greyson. He needed a transformational year.
- Find a different place to live. Though it was a wonderful place near the ocean with a secure entrance, the condo rental was always supposed to be short-term.
- Plan fun times with friends.
- Increase my drive to show love and accept God's Love.
- Help high school students—possibly start Junior Achievement at a local school.
- Volunteer at Children's Church.
- Serve or visit the elderly.
- Set up a structure for the boys.

I even set a theme for the year: *Be Still*. I had toe rings engraved with that phrase for me and my dearest friend Kristine. I wanted the ring to remind me to develop my relationship with God.

- I would go to God first.
- I would be free.
- I would be God's girl.
- I would invite God to push me to be bigger through Him. (Wow, I miss Gram.)
- I would deal with wounds from the past and be free.

Navigating health challenges didn't make the list because I still thought the bumps were inconsequential. I expected the ophthalmologist appointment in January to be a simple procedure, and I'd be done.

Dr. Kushner and his staff set me at ease as they prepared me for the surgery. The anesthesiologist put me under, and the next thing I remember was waking up to a kiss on my forehead from Dr. Kushner for being a good patient. Kristine's plane had been delayed, so seeing her in the waiting room, ready to take me home, made me feel amazing after my procedure.

Unfortunately, I had been focused on myself that morning as the boys and I got ready for our day. With the surgery weighing heavy and all the logistics that accompany a disruption in a mom's schedule, I failed to recognize the impact my surgery was having on Greyson. He struggled all day at school because he was so worried about me, so a dear friend picked him up early.

Greyson was so happy to see me when we got home. As we sat down to cuddle, he confessed, "I knew it would bleed, Mom." I thought I had hidden my uncertainty well, but my son felt it. It's important for parents going through tough circumstances to be aware that our children sense when something's off. When we don't talk with them about their fears as well as ours, they only have what they feel to work with.

Dr. Kushner called that night to check on me. I don't recall a surgeon ever doing that before. Little did I know there would be many more phone calls with Dr. Kushner as he joined this journey as a medical professional and dear friend.

I realize not everyone can relate to a cancer journey, and you may have been handed this book and wondered why it's relevant to you. This story is the testimony of one uniquely imperfect person who has found that as I've shifted away from focusing on adversity, I have had some touching moments to serve and be a light. We can all relate to adversity. If you can't connect to cancer, keep reading through the lens of an adversity you can relate to.

CHAPTER FIVE

Be Still...
Please Come Into the Office.

I was dropping the boys at school when I received the call from Dr. Kushner's office a few days later. They needed me to come into the office for biopsy results. As you might know, it is never good news when you have to go to the office after a biopsy. I held my composure and worked to wear the confident "mom mask" as I took the boys to their classrooms.

Back in the car, I called my dearest friend and let the tears flow. She offered to go with me to see Dr. Kushner, but I was determined to handle it on my own. I was committed to intentionally "Be Still," staying calm, and keep moving in confidence, so I went into the office to get a few things done before I went to the doctor's office. When I headed out for Dr. Kushner's office, I left my laptop on my desk. I anticipated returning within an hour. Life would go on as normal.

Be Still... Please Come Into the Office.

When Dr. Kushner walked by the waiting room, he saw me there and kindly escorted me to his office. I could feel his concern for my well-being as he put his hand on my shoulder to guide me to this office.

"I almost came to your house last night to give you the news, Diana," the surgeon told me as he shut his office door. "But my dear wife thought a doctor's visit at night might scare your boys."

"You have an extremely rare form of cancer in your left eye, Diana." He went on to explain the rarity of the cancer found in my left eye and the importance of going to the best place in the world for the next step in my medical journey. In fact, he had already started reaching out to the top eye hospitals.

"I've done some research and feel like you could go to one of two places. The number one eye hospital in the world is Bascom Palmer in Miami. Your other option would be the number two eye hospital in Philadelphia."

One of the nurses came in as I was processing my next move. Her hug led to tears, but I so appreciated the genuine care and concern from the staff. The doctor let me sit in his office to text my dear friend Kristine, my boss, and another dear friend, Brenda, who would rescue my son from his school issues. I wasn't ready to tell my parents.

When I left the office, I just sat in my car to balance my emotions. Kristine and I had a tear-filled conversation. Over and over, she told me, "You aren't alone." But I kept thinking, *God, I have never felt so alone.*

Despite the terrifying news, my need to make sure everyone was okay and that I didn't let anyone down shifted my focus. I started thinking about my boys and then work. My boss received the next call, and we arranged for a quick laptop pickup from work without any conversations.

At home, I started doing Google searches to research the type of cancer. The data was limited, and the tears were many. I managed to call my mom and Brenda. In between calls and tears, I tried to figure out how to solve this.

Being at home in the middle of a workday was not normal for me, and our condo required a buzzer to get in. So, when I heard someone knocking, it caught me off guard. When I opened the door, there stood Kristine's mom, Sandra. She walked in with confidence and gave me a hug.

"Diana, I have been in your shoes. I know what it feels like to get cancer news. I was praying for you, and I knew you were alone and needed a hug." Sandra prayed with me and then was gone as quickly as she'd come. Her presence helped me pivot. I moved from, "God, I can't do this. Why me?" to "God, with You, we can do this."

My boys were two-and-a-half and four at the time. I was their caregiver. They needed me to put my game face on and keep moving. That Saturday, I started planning for what might happen, including being out of work for a few months.

For many years prior to this diagnosis, I didn't want to accept help or let others in, particularly men. So, it was a bit strange when one of the vendors I dealt with at work just started to show up to help with home repairs, and I felt okay with it. The boys loved playing with Bromley and never wanted him to go. At the time, I had no idea he would become my companion on this journey.

My emotions ran high as I walked into church that next Sunday. I was reminded of the looks of sadness and pity I received from people in the congregation when I tore my ACL. I resented the looks of pity. In my journal that night, I wrote, "God, you are bigger than this." And when I dropped to my knees in prayer, I said, "I get that you are bigger than this. I know You need me to shine Your glory through this.

I need to trust and walk in You with decisions for the boys, family, and friends. Thank you."

Dr. Kushner kept in close communication with me as he talked about my case with Dr. David Tse at Bascom Palmer. Within ten days, I had an appointment with the specialist, and the sleepless nights started. Kristine took on the role of healthcare advocate as we went on one last visit with Dr. Kushner before the trip to Miami. I truly appreciate the humility and care he demonstrated acknowledging we needed someone with more expertise, as well as him caring enough to find the best solution and providing a seamless introduction.

How could I have known the trials of a failed marriage and learning to listen to a simple "Go Now" would prepare me for this trying time? I got my diagnosis nine months after my sons and I walked out of our home. As difficult as it was, the year had prepared me to walk in stillness and peace as I faced a battle in the unknown.

Reflection

Prior to my surgery in January, I certainly didn't realize how easy it was compared to what was to come. I am thankful for Florida Health Care Ophthalmology. When I told friends and family about my experience and how much Dr. Kushner and his team guided, helped, and encouraged me along the way, they were amazed. Patients at other facilities don't receive that level of care, commitment, and friendship. Not every patient walks in the door with a smile and a positive mindset.

As I reflect on the impactful phone call and quick life pivot, I am touched by the friends and family that stepped in.

Sandra's few moments of encouragement sparked me to shift to hope and purpose. We need each other. Dear Dr. Kushner went the extra mile to care for me and ensure the best solution. We complete our jobs because we have to. But a calling gives us an opportunity to impact lives. Let's reflect together:

- Who has stepped in to be a "Sandra" in the most difficult times for you?
- What mindset do you carry into troubling times?
- When a friend or acquaintance gets difficult news, what is your normal response? Do you encourage them or frustrate them?

Application

- Thank the "Sandra's" in your life with a call, a note, or even a text.
- Observe people around you who need a Sandra. Don't miss your opportunity to be one. Our adversities can uniquely qualify us to add value to another.
- At your next doctor's appointment or when you face adversity, choose to walk in with a positive mindset, thinking about how you can show kindness and care. See what opportunities come your way.

CHAPTER SIX

Is It in My Brain?

With an appointment in Miami on the books, life moved into fast-forward. I had to shift my focus from my role as a mom to me first. Dear friends stepped in to care for the boys, and I headed to Miami with Kristine.

The Daytona hospitals seemed small compared to the Bascom Palmer UHealth campus in downtown Miami. The next few days promised to be long, but we were prepared to go with the flow. Nothing mattered except the time I spent with the experts.

We checked in at the hospital and waited for the next steps. Today, I have the routine down, but that first visit felt a bit foreign. First, the optician's assistant took me back to check my vision. Then, the doctor performed his exam. Since UHealth is a teaching hospital, multiple fellows looked into and felt around my eye.

When each one completed his or her probe, Dr. Tse told us he was unsure about the diagnosis. He wanted to see a fresh MRI. So, I got an appointment for that evening, and we headed back to the hotel.

If you aren't familiar with Miami, an MRI at 8:30 p.m. may sound minor. However, the hospital district sits in an area with many homeless. And while the streets where the hotel was located were lovely, the nighttime drive quickly turned from well-lit and pristine to precarious and dark. A bit nervous about navigating at night, Kristine and I left plenty of time for the drive.

I had multiple MRIs for my ACL injuries, but this was the first with an IV contrast. I'm happy to report that, in my experience, MRIs are not as bad as people think. I like to look at them as a time to rest. Of course, as I've said before, your mindset going in will directly impact your experience.

After they got the IV in—I'd been dreading that part—and I chose my music, it was time to begin. My favorite tunes helped overshadow the banging of the machine, and I laid back to rest.

In my journal that night, I wrote about how this journey was challenging my standard of showing compassion to others. Until you begin a journey like this, it's hard to truly understand how it will affect you. I ended my journal entry with, "Your will be done, and may I bet at peace with it."

By 8:30 the next morning, we were back at Bascom Palmer. Dr. Tse drew several examples of the eye and cancer on a small piece of paper. He used a metaphor that Kristine and I will never forget. "Diana, this type of cancer is like marbles dropping on the floor. One never knows where all the marbles will roll."

The bump on the corner of my eye had white cancerous lumps, and the MRI confirmed another behind my eye. My greatest fear began to surface. *Is it in my brain?* Dr. Tse led us to the hallway to review the images. "Your brain is good. No signs of a tumor." Perhaps you can imagine my relief. He told us the next step would be a biopsy.

We had to wait a couple of hours for the next procedure, so we went for coffee, and I called Dr. Kushner with the update.

Dr. Tse told us the biopsy wouldn't require any sedation. The thought of being fully awake made me chuckle inwardly; I thought twilight sedation in January was going to be tough. A kind nurse named Denise used an ointment to numb the area and tested the numbness a few times before Dr. Tse came in. I held her hand and a stress ball as I followed instructions to move my eye around, and Dr. Tse took multiple samples. They told me the worst part of the procedure would be removing the mask to cover my right eye. I smiled as I let them know I didn't agree. Though I didn't experience any pain, it was strange and uncomfortable hearing the snips yet not feeling them, smelling the burning, and not feeling it.

Surgery would be scheduled quickly; however, the biopsy would determine the extent of the operation. We could have waited in Miami for the results, but I wanted to head home. The boys were so happy to see me, and Bromley came by to help me with car seats and hear about my day.

I spent the next few days wondering about the biopsy and caring for two bouncy boys. My journal was a mix of emotions from "God, I'm pissed I have cancer in my eye" to "God, I've always had a dream to write and be a speaker. Is this the time?"

Notes of encouragement, prayer, and offers to help flooded my mailbox. I had no idea what help I needed. My prayers kept returning to "God, please help me hear from you. Help me be a light for You in this. Is there a purpose in all this? I don't want to let You down. I know You can't use me when I'm feeling sorry for myself. You are bigger than my problems."

Being able to shift back into mom mode was a blessed distraction. Bromley had become a trusted friend by now, but when he invited us to come to his ex-wife's house so the boys could play and I could relax, it seemed odd on so many levels. I prayed as I sat on the floor of my condo. "God, am I supposed to do this? Bromley has been a friend, and the distraction would be good, but should I accept?"

The boys loved the thought of a new adventure. They spent the evening playing and having fun, but when we left, I knew I needed to guard my heart.

I knew keeping our routine would be good for the boys. That meant we got up early on Sunday for breakfast at Panera with my cousin Bryan and then went on to church. There, the pastor's wife asked if I wanted to go forward for prayer and to be anointed. This was new territory for me. Yes, I grew up in the church. But I'd spent very little time at the altar and the anointment part … ? I said yes if she would go with me.

My single mom's class greeted me with hugs and made me think of Gram as they complimented me on my poise, smile, and calmness. Many of these ladies are dear friends to this day, and the journey we started as single moms of small children has continued into their teens.

On Monday morning, Bascom Palmer called with a surgery date, and on Tuesday, Dr. Tse called with biopsy results. The cancer was also in the upper eyelid. My surgery date probably needed to be moved up. As much as I disliked the unknown, it had become a standard part of my life. I had no choice but to learn to accept it, trust Dr. Tse with the right timing, and believe that God had every person and area in the situation under control.

As I waited for my parents to arrive from Pennsylvania, I reflected on the past year. Twelve months ago, I met with the boy's dad to let him know we needed to part ways. Now, as another Valentine's Day approached, I found myself hugging my boys more while I balanced the news of cancer and surgery and watched my parents deal with the pain.

I spent as much time as possible with the boys. Parenting kept me busy and focused on them. But when I had alone time, my mind wandered to places it shouldn't go. *What if I don't wake up from surgery? What if I'm not the same mentally? How can I prepare my friends and family?* I wondered what my worry sounded like to God. Was I not trusting Him?

At times, the barrage of questions from caring people overwhelmed me. My nature is to take care of others and keep them happy. I appreciated their care, but I really just wanted to send a bulk status update. I didn't want to have to constantly repeat the same scary message. The attention felt like the squawking birds that often flew into my window at work. The multitude of questions throughout the day wore on my soul and my mental state, like the sound of those birds continuously crashing into my window.

I already shared how I like to be in control and make decisions so I can keep up with what is next. This growing period taught me that I can move forward with only what I know today. On that day, I knew only one thing: I had cancer near my left eye, with surgery scheduled in a week. What would happen after surgery, I had to leave it in God's hands.

As I prepared for surgery and an extended period away from my boys, I balanced the "what ifs" by making time for photos with my boys. I didn't know what would happen in the next few months, and I needed these photo memories for them and for me. The unknown loomed large in front of me. Yes, I could have asked questions about what I would look like after surgery and how long the healing would take. I had a huge list of whats and whens. Yet, I knew I needed to walk into this uncharted territory choosing to trust the medical team God had blessed me with.

Reflection

Many times, adversity and medical challenges cause individuals to walk away from the church. My time of struggle came while I was learning what a church family meant as a single mom with two young boys. It helped me to move closer to the congregation I worshiped with. I learned to share my news and allow people to get close as they extended a hand to help and prayed for me and my family. Two boys limit a person's quiet time. And though I journaled through the difficulty, I wish I had taken more time to write out my thoughts.

Prior to this, the only surgeon I trusted was the one who operated on my knee. But that adventure was minor compared to this new journey of unknowns. I spent many years keeping tough times to myself and putting my guard up. This era was different. No external guard could hide the impacts of the surgery. I had to learn to be more open and transparent about the journey.

Looking back, I realized I learned a lot about how to be present for someone else going through a massive life transformation. I also discovered everyone goes through times when they need to give themselves permission to be "me-focused" for a short while. We don't want to stay in that place; however, some of us need that nod of approval before we let ourselves go to a place of "me first."

- Do you know anyone receiving tough medical news? What is your approach to communicating with them?
- What are some tough times you have navigated through that you didn't think you could handle?

Application

- In my early mom days, my journal time was often disjointed, yet I can still read my notes and remember. Take time each day to reflect, express gratitude, and stretch your soul. What time will you choose?
- Be conscious of how you respond to a friend or family member getting tough medical news. Consider how you can enter a conversation in a way that gives them room to share without focusing on their diagnosis or problem. Think about how you can show care without being a "squawking bird."

CHAPTER SEVEN

Joy Along the Journey

The Friday before my surgery, I wrapped up things at work, preparing to be off for a month. Then, on Saturday, I gave my boys a hug goodbye as they headed for Pennsylvania. Now, I could focus on preparing for surgery. But how do you prepare for the unknown?

I started Sunday morning with a view of the sunrise over the ocean from my condominium balcony; the colors were so beautiful. I sat in awe and pondered all I had to be thankful for—my parents stepping in to care for my boys, my church family, my dear friend Kristine, my family, and my friend Bromley. I jotted in my journal that I was uncertain why Bromley stepped in to help me, and I needed to accept help.

My cousin Bryan joined me at church on Sunday. I attended the early service with the more senior generation. My grandparents sparked a special place in my heart for these more mature saints and gave me the desire to join with the generations that walked before me. That Sunday, the pastor asked me to come forward so they could pray for me. I was humbled by the number of people who gathered around to pray for me.

After church, I waited patiently for the call that it was time to head to South Florida. Kristine was not able to travel a day early, but my heart really wanted to take time to stop in West Palm to see friends and have some fun before the surgery. Many times, I chose to mix fun in on the journey. I've spent time looking for different places to stay, walk, and eat so I could enjoy the experience beyond the doctor's visits.

My new friend Bromley offered to drive so I could visit friends in West Palm and have a mini vacation to distract me from what lay ahead. I hesitantly accepted. After my journey over the past few years and two unsuccessful marriages, I had built barriers that didn't allow me to accept kindness from men, even friends. Our ride was filled with conversation including a few surrounding the walls we both had put around our hearts.

Priscilla and I had been friends when I lived in Palm Beach, and we often met halfway for pedicures and shopping. I was glad she could join us for dinner at City Walk, followed by a nice walk. It was fun to catch up and tell stories. She passed hugs all around as she said goodbye. On the way back to the hotel, I made a mental note that though Bromley had never hugged me mid-crisis, he freely embraced my friend he just met.

The thirty-minute walk back to the hotel spurred many memories. We passed the apartments I lived in for three years while I worked at Palm Beach Atlantic and traveled along familiar Flagler Avenue and the Intracoastal.

At the hotel, Bromley and I headed to our rooms on opposite sides of the building. I was determined to not accept free assistance, so I paid for both hotel rooms and arranged for their locations. Inside my room, the silence became a bit overwhelming. I couldn't sleep. With tears, I sat there, attempting to unravel the unknown and figure out the future. As always, I wanted to take charge of what was way beyond my control.

I had lived in Palm Beach for four years and never made a point to get up to see the sunrise. I guess we take for granted what's always there. This time, I rose early. I needed the sun's reminder of God's beauty and presence. Sitting on the beach, I reflected on the magnificent view and rested in the peace I found in the early morning rays.

Back at the hotel, Bromley and I walked around a bit and ate breakfast at one of my favorite restaurants before heading to meet Kristine. She looked uncertain as she drove up beside us. Kristine hadn't met Bromley yet, and her protective nature questioned his intentions. I wasn't sure he noticed she gave him a courteous greeting and then quickly said goodbye to whisk me off to Miami for surgery preparations.

Surgery Day

I woke early on the day of my surgery to journal. The many texts, calls, and Facebook messages offering encouragement and prayer were overwhelming. Bascom Palmer performed only same-day procedures; nevertheless, their care, kindness, and thoroughness were impressive. When they called me to prep for surgery, I gave Kristine a big hug and followed the attendant.

As I donned my lovely gown, purple cap, and socks, Dr. Tse's fellow came in and asked, "What are you here for today?" As a rookie patient, I didn't quite get why he was asking me what the plan was for surgery. Later, I realized it was a part of protocol to ensure the patient was informed. At that moment, I only hoped he knew.

But then he pulled out his marker and made a purple X by my left eye—a quality measure I came to appreciate over the years. Next, Dr. Tse stopped to visit to warn me I may experience double vision and other irritations until the surgery series was complete. And finally, the anesthesiologist came.

A seventy-year-old lady named Yolanda was in the bed beside me during prep. I heard her tell the nurse that she was there all alone. Her kids were distant. I seized the opportunity to talk with her and help ease her mind about her surgery.

I learned a valuable lesson during this surgery—strong painkillers don't agree with me. I thought asking for anti-nausea meds in my IV would help alleviate the vomiting, but it only did the trick for the first hour after I woke from surgery. I managed to talk with Dr. Tse briefly before the Dilaudid kicked in. Kristine was beyond concerned and tried to convince the nurses I needed to spend the night. But they stuck to protocol, and after hours of waiting for my stomach to settle, at 9:30 p.m., we headed for the hotel.

The next morning, Kristine drove me home, and from that day on, the ride home from Bascom Palmer always included a nap. Kristine needed to go home to be with her family, so Bromley met us at my condo. After my friend left, Bromley walked with me to get my mail. I quickly discovered I would have to learn how to maneuver with one eye for a few weeks. I missed the elevator button, and I could not sync the key with the keyhole to open the mailbox. Thankfully,

Gram taught me to laugh along the journey. I developed a new appreciation for the Creator's handiwork on eyes and how they function as I learned to navigate in monovision.

I couldn't wash my own hair for a few days, and Bromley kindly scheduled a hair appointment. Dinners out and other little excursions were a great distraction for me, and I provided entertainment to any crowd we were in. More than a few leered at Bromley, and we guessed they assumed he beat me. Not only did I have an eye covered, I also had a nice battered-wife-looking bruise popping up.

The first Sunday after surgery, my dear friend Robyn and her two daughters picked me up for church. The girls held my hand to guide me. I could see enough to walk, but God was teaching me to accept the care and concern of others.

Surgery Number Two

A week after surgery, Kristine and I headed back to Miami for a check-up. Yolanda was in the waiting room calling people to tell them about her cancer. It was sad listening to her fight her battle alone. I walked over to sit with her, gave her a hug, and invited her to come sit with Kristine and me.

When Dr. Tse and his associate Dr. Ko opened my eye, I had to blink a few times before I could see again. The eye chart was a bit blurry at first, but I could see. The photos of the cancer revealed a tumor I thought looked too big to be inside my head—1.5 centimeters. He told me they had gone as deep as they could to get clean margins.

The biopsy they took from near my nose bone was negative; however, the one they took from my eyelid still tested positive. I needed another surgery. Thankfully, Dr. Tse's first choice of the next day was not feasible. Instead, we scheduled it for Thursday. I had a few more days to prepare.

As I listened to the doctors talk about the skin needed to repair the eyelid, I started to tear up. They talked about the possibility of using some of my right eyelid. I couldn't lose use of that eye, too. Dr. Tse saw my concern and explained the option of using the roof of my mouth.

The next steps still sounded daunting. I would arrive at Dr. Tse's office early Thursday morning for an in-office biopsy procedure so he could identify the clean margin. Then we would head to the operating room, where he would use skin from the roof of my mouth to fill in my eyelid. It sounded so pleasant.

We headed back to Daytona to sleep in our own beds for a couple of days, and I updated my family and friends on the news. Going into an empty house was sad at times. I could talk with my boys, yet it wasn't the same as hugging and holding them. They enjoyed time with Grandma and Pappy, yet I missed them so much. At that point, I hadn't thought to ask how long my left eye would be closed after surgery. It was enough to know the next step.

The day before surgery, Bromley took me to visit with Dr. Kushner. He provided insight on what to expect. I asked him about driving with one eye. I wanted to stay as independent as possible. He assured me people drive with one eye all the time. I would just need some practice.

Later that evening, Bromley drove me to West Palm Beach to have dinner with my friends Priscilla and Abel. It was so helpful to visit friends on the way to Miami.

I had to be at Dr. Tse's office by eight the next morning. Another fun biopsy procedure while I was awake. Thankfully, Denise and her team always helped distract me from the large numbing needle. After the biopsy, I had to wait about an hour while the margins were evaluated, and then it was time to prepare for surgery.

Kristine made it to the hospital before surgery and stayed with me until the anesthesia team came. I teared up when the anesthesiologist told me they may not put me fully under. Twilight anesthesia did not sound pleasant when they talked about taking part of the roof of my mouth. Dr. Tse assured me they would monitor me and keep me comfortable.

Even with only twilight anesthesia, I fell asleep. I woke up terribly groggy with packing in my mouth, but I didn't feel ill this time.

Brushing my teeth with the packing in my mouth made me nervous. Thankfully, the hotel was only a few miles from Bascom Palmer. I spent the first night of many sleeping propped up on pillows to avoid rolling onto the surgical area.

The next morning, Dr. Tse reviewed the surgery site and cleared me to head back home.

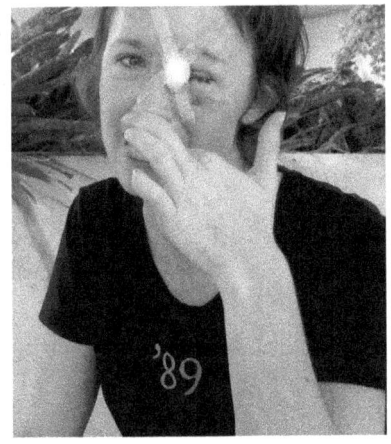

My new look was quite amazing. Bromley received even more judgemental looks when we went out. To lighten the mood, we shopped for pirate patches. Not only would they cover the wound and block out the light, but hopefully, they would minimize the concerned looks.

I started to count down the days until I could pick up my boys and my one-eye driving lessons began. I'm sure nearly everyone takes the human eyes and their connectivity to the brain for granted. Normally, our eyes just work. My temporary eye closure led to a whole new appreciation of the intricacy of God's design.

It is wonderful how the brain can adjust to coordinate with one eye. The patch helped create a blackout and allowed my left eye to rest.

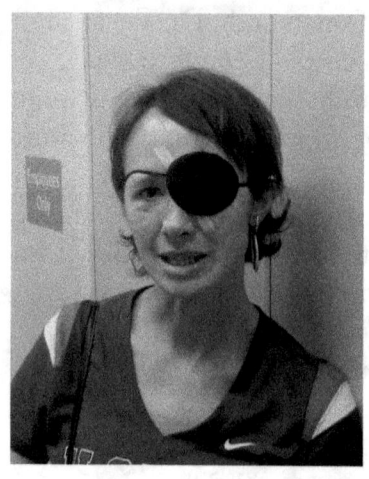

I had one more trip to Miami before life could get back to somewhat normal. My driving skills weren't quite ready for that kind of road trip, so I asked for help. My cousin Bryan drove me halfway, where we met Priscilla, who took me as far as Palm Beach. Then Kristine met me for dinner and carried me the rest of the trip. Over and over, I learned lessons on relying on others to help me through this season.

The surgeon had good news. Everything looked great. But the longer he talked, the more shocking comments he shared.

"Be careful with your mouth for two weeks, and watch what you eat. You don't want too much pressure in your mouth." Dr. Tse continued, "You will need to keep your eye closed for one to three months."

One to three months … That took a minute to process. I never imagined it would need to stay closed so long after surgery. I finally decided since I'm a stellar patient I would plan on one month.

Reflection

Perspective is everything. I often approach life by focusing on what I have to do. Inserting fun and visits with friends on the way to Miami helped shift my mindset to what I get to do. Sitting beside patients like Yolanda, who had no one by their side, helped me see through a different lens. I started to look for those who needed kindness in the waiting room. My knee surgeries in college seemed major at the time. But my current situation helped me shift the definition of a "Knock My Socks Off" moment.

Many life experiences prepare us for what is to come. I expected my eye to be closed for one week but had to face months. Arguing for a shorter patch time was not an option. I had to make a choice about my mindset. Within a day of only using one eye, I became more appreciative than ever of my vision. I also learned to laugh about the random stares and the many snafus related to the one-eye adjustment. Reflecting on these questions can help us find joy in our journey.

- What do you need to pause and be thankful for?
- What has felt so big at the moment (for example, an eye forced closed for months) that ended up being a blessing or a minor obstacle?
- Where do you need to find the fun and create laughter?

Application

- I remember laughing at the stares when I had my bruised eye taped up. Not everyone can laugh at what they are navigating. Is there someone in your life who is struggling with a disability or appearance change that could use some empathy or encouragement?

- What obstacle or unexpected impact has caused you to freeze? What can you do today to move on?

CHAPTER EIGHT

Back to Normal

As I prepared to pick up the boys with Bromley's help, my mind began to make the shift from taking care of me to the boys' schedule and balancing healing and being a mom. I looked forward to life returning to normal.

My devotional gave me an appropriate reminder the morning we headed out to meet the boys. "The Best Is Yet to Come" was the theme for the day. Life around my fortieth birthday hadn't looked anything like I anticipated. I liked the thought of better days coming.

My parents had taken the boys to Edisto Beach, South Carolina, and Bromley graciously offered to drive the five hours to pick them up. The boys greeted me with big hugs. Greyson had a few questions, but Ben was just happy to be with me. And this man willing to drive ten hours to help me get my boys back home peaked my Mom and Dad's curiosity. After a short visit, we headed back to Daytona Beach, hoping to get back home at a reasonable hour.

Back to Normal

Dinner at Cracker Barrel proved tougher than I anticipated with the boys. So, once again, I had to accept help as I entered the new waters of keeping two active boys safe with one eye.

As we pulled into the condo parking garage, my mouth started bleeding. I'm so glad Bromley was there to help me and the boys get upstairs. It's hard to explain my feeling of helplessness. The roof of my mouth was gushing blood. Switching between ice packs and salt water in my mouth to stop the bleeding, I had to stay calm so my boys didn't get scared.

I found myself questioning God. "Okay, I've accepted the eye. Why the mouth? And why now? The boys are just getting home to me."

On Sunday morning, I woke early to reflect on the day and prepare to be a mom again. Unfortunately, it wasn't long before the intense bleeding started again. I texted Dr. Kushner and Dr. St. James for guidance. Both recommended I get to the ER.

My cousin Bryan rescued me and took the boys to church. He then coordinated with Robyn to take care of them that night. So many angels supported me in the whirlwind.

I went to the hospital thinking they would just quickly do some magic to stop the bleeding. Instead, after a few views of my mouth, they admitted me for emergency surgery. The graft was too close to a vessel, creating an avenue for blood loss. Bromley waited patiently while I went through surgery.

When I woke, a nurse informed me I had lost a lot of blood, so I'd have to spend the night. But my mom instincts immediately kicked in. I needed to be with my boys. They just got home. Bromley tells the story with much more animation than I do. I had my mom hat on, and I was not going to be separated from them without a fight.

You probably already guessed that I lost that battle.

As Bromley and Kristine headed for the car, the nurse looked at me and smiled. "Your husband really loves you. I can see it in his eyes."

"Hmm," I responded. "He is not my husband. We are just friends."

"He will be someday. Look at those eyes. He loves you."

Bromley and Kristine were back first thing in the morning to check on me, and another friend stepped in to help with the boys. Thankfully, I was released the next day with some packing in my mouth to stop the bleeding and some tips to manage the pain. I was blessed that many friends stepped in to care for the boys despite my desire to be the mom who didn't need help.

Ironically, I believed I would be able to be somewhat independent and care for my boys. This setback was just another humble reminder to trust God and accept the help of friends and family.

As I reflected on my state of mind, I realized I owed a big thank you to my dear friends who stepped in to help and save the day. I truly appreciated our dear sitter, Amanda. She helped me with the boys as I balanced the mouth pain, navigating with one eye and learning humility.

Greyson struggled in preschool before my surgery, so I worried about how missing a few weeks might affect him. I made a point to have lunch with him to give him more assurance, and we celebrated the green days at school. Green days for a preschooler meant a full day without any behavior or respect issues with teachers and classmates.

One More Scare

Sleep started to be a challenge again as I balanced returning to work and parenting. Mornings went from easy to chaotic and stressful. Getting two boys ready, taking them to school, and taking myself to work was stressful. At the same time, I signed up for a forty-day Lenten challenge. Maybe this wasn't the best time to add additional goals for myself.

My parents came to town, and we visited with them in their Ocean Walk room. Mom and Dad offered to take them back to Pennsylvania, yet I needed and wanted to be a present mom. I struggled to remain stern with the boys as I dealt with my personal pain. My questions for God sounded like this:

- God, how do I be a better mom?
- Am I sending them to Pennsylvania for the wrong reason?
- How can I be better at organizing them and my schedule?

The boys stayed with Mom and Dad for another night at Ocean Walk, which gave me time to think. And a check-in with Dr. Kushner told me the eye and mouth were both healing well.

My range of emotions was intense when I was alone at night. The future held so many unknowns, and I still had that prominent desire to control what I could. Every once in a while, I hit a low point in the evenings after the boys went to bed. I would sit and type while the tears flowed. At times, establishing consequences and discipline with my strong-willed Greyson became really hard, causing me to cry as I tried to hold strong.

The boys ended up staying in Florida. But as I moved from frustration to the desire to improve, I received another medical surprise. When drying Benny after his bath, he was being silly and bumped my nose by accident.

Dr. Tse told me he had to remove a tear duct and insert a temporary drain. I just had no idea that this fishing line-type contraception was hooked through my nose and into my eye for the tear duct to drain. I found out what it looked like as it fell onto the counter. Panic set in. *Would I need another surgery?*

Within a few days, Dr. Tse alleviated my fears. The loss of the drain was a non-issue. I would experience drainage since I didn't have functioning tear ducts anymore, but it wouldn't cause damage. How many times had I taken my tear ducts for granted? It soon became a joke that I was the only person who could continually cry out of one eye. The water just poured out during allergy season.

No sooner had I maneuvered that medical tragedy than the next heartbreak happened. The church preschool called to ask me to come get Greyson. They were kicking him out.

Because I was in the middle of several local doctor appointments, my friend Misty offered to keep Greyson with her. The ordeal left part of me wondering why a church ministry preschool couldn't be more helpful during this season, while the other part felt blessed that the ladies in the church stepped in to help me and pour love into Greyson. That's when I realized I had missed the cues that this wasn't the right preschool for him.

Now, I had to find a new preschool for Greyson and take a trip to Miami to check on my progress. I was so grateful for Brenda and the others who stepped in to help me with Greyson and Ben.

I felt like a failure. Thoughts of things I could have done better overwhelmed me. I hadn't worked with him enough. I let my eye distract me and missed moments with Greyson.

With the different stresses, I nearly forgot to enjoy the time with my boys and life in general. What did normal life used to feel like? Finally, one Saturday morning felt like the pre-cancer days. We woke up late, made muffins, went to the YMCA, and had fun playing together. It felt so normal; I found myself on the I95 ramp just like before. A slight panic set in as I realized I had not taken an interstate with one eye yet. But we made it home with no problems!

Emotions ran high as I tried to figure out how to be a mom, executive, and friend again. Many days, I felt completely unqualified.

On top of that, despite being closed and patched, my left eye still wanted to work. I started to experience dizziness and disorientation, which was a bit scary, particularly as a single mom. A CT scan reassured me that all was well.

Many days, I wrote in my journal, "God, am I the parent You want me to be?" It was difficult to balance all the aspects of life. Still, I truly wanted to be extremely grateful and a blessing to others.

At the end of April 2014, my cousin drove me to Miami for another follow-up appointment. We took Greyson along for the ride to prevent a bad day at school. Everything was healing well, but the stitches and the lens protecting my eye had to stay. I asked about the tear duct, but Dr. Tse reminded me it would be years before we would repair the tear duct. Repair would require drilling a hole in my nose bone, giving any remaining cancer cells a path to grow. I would take "tears" pouring out of my eye rather than cancer in my nose.

I tried to treasure the fun times with my two sweet boys, but I have to admit I was thankful that Mom and Dad were coming for Greyson's preschool graduation and planned to take them to Pennsylvania for a few weeks.

Greyson's graduation was a huge blessing, and the weight lifted off my shoulders after navigating a year he certainly didn't understand. As the boys prepared to go with their grandparents, I realized there was no normal. Life continues to evolve, kids keep growing, and fun times and obstacles come and go. All we can do is live and be present in each moment.

Reflection

The title of this book echoes throughout my life—Uniquely Imperfect, Uniquely Qualified. I was an imperfect parent. I missed moments with my boys and could have made better choices and gone in better directions. In reality, we will all make mistakes in parenting, life, business, and so on. How we respond to those mistakes—whether we blame others or take responsibility and learn from them with a positive mindset—makes the difference in the trajectory of one's life.

Like me, many want to fly solo. The independent part of me wanted to reject the kindness and love people wanted to pour out. God kept humbling me and reminding me to allow others to step in and be kind. My desire to be in control had to shift as the cancer moved many things well beyond my control. Some days, it felt like everything was piling up. I often wrote in my journal, "Okay God, Okay God, I've accepted the eye. Why … ? Why my mouth? Why is Greyson having such a difficult time?"

- At times, we'll have to fight to choose gratitude and joy. I remember how helpless I felt with blood pouring out of my mouth. I had no choice but to humbly ask and allow others to help me. Complaining would not help with the outcome. Of course, in my case, it's hard to complain with blood pouring out of your mouth.
- Greyson's change in preschool was frustrating on so many levels. I felt most disappointed in myself. I missed the cues. I was distracted and not connected to what I needed to do that day.

Application

- When tough things happen, it's easier to blame others or situations and move on without any application or transformation. I could have blamed my son's school behavior challenges on the teacher and ignored the behavior at home. But that approach of placing blame would not have helped Greyson to be the young man he is today. God gave me multiple prompts to improve in parenting. Self-reflection caused me to realize I needed to act more. What areas are you placing the fault on others and missing your opportunity to act?

CHAPTER NINE

More Lessons on the Journey

I looked forward to seeing the sunrise on the water while the boys visited Mom and Dad. A few days after they left, Bromley brought his boat to the dock at my condominium. With my journal and Bible in hand, I was prepared to be on the water while Bromley fished and we waited for the sunrise.

As I neared the boat, Bromley suggested I sit on the dock and slide into the boat. "It's a far drop," he said. I didn't pause and proceeded to step into the boat with confidence. Unfortunately, Bromley was right; it was much more than a step, it was a leap. My right foot made the first impact, and then I banged my ribs on the cooler intended for the fresh catch. The pain was a bit intense, and the fall took my breath. Bromley squatted beside me. "Please talk. Say something." I eventually found enough breath to speak, "I'm fine. I just need to sit for a while."

Pride ruled. "Let's keep going. I'll feel better in a few minutes."

More Lessons on the Journey

I thought I was tough, but as soon as the pain became more and more intense, I realized the pain was tougher. Bromley didn't catch any fish. Instead, we headed back to the dock, and he gently and quite slowly helped me out of the boat. He probably felt like it took me an hour to get in the truck. With every move, the pain grew more intense, particularly in my ribs.

With my eye still sewn shut, I found myself back in the emergency room. I didn't have a simple broken rib. No, I broke multiple bones in my foot and cracked several ribs. Crutches were out of the question. I found myself humbled one more time with a walker to keep me upright because crutches don't work well with fractured ribs.

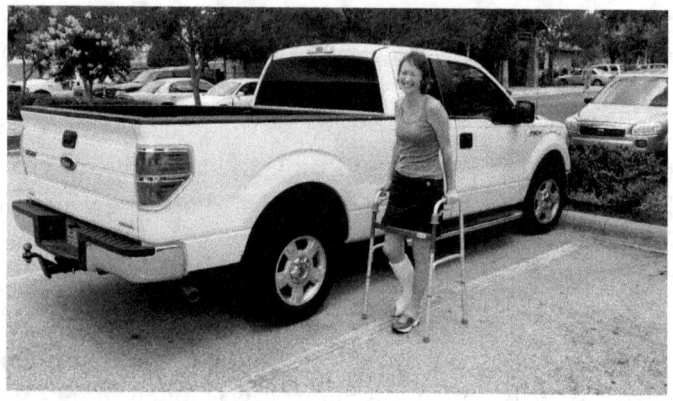

Early into my cancer journey, my unique and imperfect look became a topic of every doctor's appointment. Even the orthopedic surgeon inquired about my eye and its unique appearance when I went for my follow-up. He also cautioned against flying until the cast was off—just one more hiccup. I had planned to fly to pick up the boys, and I found out later, a surprise fortieth birthday party awaited me. I was not going to make the trip or the party.

Uniquely Imperfect, Uniquely Qualified

As you might have guessed, by this time, my relationship with Bromley had started to move beyond friendship as he proved to be a trusted friend, significant other, and caregiver. A week after my foot and rib injury, he drove me to West Palm Beach for a follow-up appointment with Dr. Tse. Though Dr. Tse was a bit more clinical than Dr. Kushner, he had become a trusted mentor for this journey.

Stopping to visit friends had become a wonderful bright spot in each trip to visit the doctor. I warned them that I added a cast and a walker to my unique look. And Priscilla helped promote the uniqueness with a lovely handmade eyepatch. The night was filled with rib-splitting laughter—worth every moment of the pain.

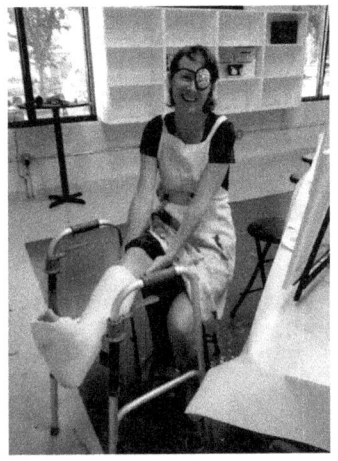

My new, unique look earned me a "fall risk" bracelet from the nurses when I checked in with Dr. Tse's team and a multitude of questions and opportunities to share my story before they moved me to the same-day surgery room.

The numbing needle created some intense sensations this time and took a bit longer than usual to take effect. As I waited I couldn't help but wonder what it would feel like without the stitches and contraptions. *Would my eye work?*

Hearing the snipping and feeling the "conformer" being peeled off was still a bit unnerving. Even numb, it felt like a sticker being removed from my eyeball. It was no more pleasant than the swab they took for the first biopsy. But after a few blinks, relief replaced the nervousness because I could see out of my left eye. After being restricted for so long, the muscles would take some time to regain full movement.

"We will see you in one month and do a biopsy on your other eye just to be safe." Dr. Tse's words were encouraging and comforting.

The month of June seemed to take forever without the boys. I missed them so much. Tears welled up every time I called and heard Benny ask about my boo-boo and tell me he wanted to sit on my lap. I had to stay focused on the blessing of having time to spend alone and with friends.

With all of June's slowness, it brought good news at the end. The biopsy swab from the eye opening was negative. So far, all was good.

Though I could see three-dimensionally again, the injury to my right foot meant no driving. Thankfully, Bromley drove me to meet my parents and boys halfway. The new look caused the boys a little hesitation at first, but it was quickly overlooked.

At home, the boys were quick to help. Plus, they loved the additional medical supplies. Ben thought testing the spirometer was a wonderful challenge. Additionally, Aunt Sarah visited to help with driving and keeping life balanced for the boys.

As I kept adding new realities to our adventure, I started to understand how difficult these transitions of spending time away from home and having so many visitors felt for Greyson and Benjamin. On top of the eye, the foot, the ribs, the walker, and having to learn how to accept help, I had to figure out a way to graciously take parenting advice from those who weren't parents. God had more lessons for me to learn.

My cast came off the day before Ben's birthday, allowing me to drive again. The day after Ben's birthday, Bromley and I headed back to Palm Beach for the procedure on my right eye.

I seldom had to wait in Dr. Tse's office, but on this day, another procedure was taking a bit longer, so I had to just lay there listening to the beeps of the machines. I really just wanted some quiet.

I found myself filled with gratitude as Dr. Tse came into the room. I knew that big needle would be headed toward my good eye in just a moment. I was blessed to have a doctor I felt comfortable with. It takes a tremendous level of trust and peace from God to watch a needle that size come toward your eye and stay still.

Within a week, the call came. The biopsy on my right eye was clear. *God, was it time to settle back to normal?* With the cast off and both eyes clear, we headed out for a family vacation in Branson. The boys got to build bonds with their cousins and spend time with aunts and uncles. The trip was a huge blessing, filled with some moments of laughter.

My brother stopped to check on us one day at our unit. After a few knocks, I answered the door. He looked at me and asked, "Something looks off with your left eye. Are you okay?" I tried to stay stoic and give a lighthearted remark that a few surgeries may have impacted my eye. It was a blessing to be able to laugh about it.

As the summer flew by, Kristine decided to throw a fortieth-birthday party for me. I never know who to invite or how the party should evolve when it's centered around me, but my soul sister Kristine stepped in and took care of all the details. The past year had not panned as I expected, so I was incredibly blessed to celebrate with the people who supported me along the journey.

I continued to receive good news from the doctors, so it was time to focus on Greyson starting kindergarten. It's hard to describe the pressure I felt as a mom to be patient and kind when his behavior escalated. I prayed frequently for God's wisdom and judgment, and my journal was full of questions about guidance, parenting, patience, and peace.

Those watching from the outside complimented me as a mother, a positive person through life's challenges, and a hero of the faith. Many days, I didn't feel worthy of the kind words. Still, I was blessed and teary from the compliments.

Reflection

We all have tough seasons to go through, and we each have to choose how we will respond to the tough seasons. Within weeks of the left eye being opened again, I failed to listen and added on another adversity—broken ribs and a broken foot. It would have been easy to place blame, yet it would not have contributed to moving forward and learning from the pain. Not only was the pain physical, but it was also painful for my independent persona to continue to need help.

- My summer was disrupted greatly because I failed to listen to wise advice to pause, sit, and ease into the boat. Pride jumped in, and it left me with a painful reminder to pause and listen. Where have you felt pain because you didn't pause to listen to a friend extending a hand?

Application

- Relationships flourish when we swallow our pride and don't allow it to get in the way. Relationships struggle when pride is more important than humility. Where in your life is pride winning? What action can you take to substitute humility for pride?
- The night with friends was filled with so much laughter it increased the pain in my ribs. But it was worth it. Where do you need to lighten up and just laugh?

CHAPTER TEN

The End of the Year of 40... Missed the Mark

As December rolled in, I found myself reflecting on my parenting. Did I set a good leadership example? Did my boys understand what it means to be a child of God and a good friend? Where did the year go? The mission trip had gone on without me, and I couldn't be sure I made progress as a mom.

I certainly learned to be more proactive with school notes or messages and to step in to fight for Greyson and understand him better. I need to be happy with progress, not perfection.

Christmas with the family in Pennsylvania was a blessing. We pretended Santa came to Pap's house. The boys were so excited. They opened presents and danced around the tree. I was overjoyed that my left eye healed tremendously. People I hadn't seen for six months had no idea what I had gone through. To anyone who hadn't seen me since last Christmas, I looked pretty much the same.

Traditionally, I fly back after Christmas, and the boys stay with Mom and Dad for a week. They enjoy the cold weather and a trip to the Pennsylvania Farm Show, and I get some quiet reflection time as well as a New Year's Eve outing with friends.

This year during my time of reflection, I looked over the bucket list I had created last New Year's. It obviously didn't pan out as I had hoped, yet the blessings were abundant, and the lessons were beyond impactful.

On January 9, I got a final sigh of relief. Dr. Tse stated with confidence I was still cancer-free. As much as I didn't want more appointments, over the past year, I learned transparency was the best course of action. Dr. Tse hadn't ordered any scans. He had performed a routine review of my eye. Even with his behind-the-eye exam and the way he palpated the area where the cancer had been, I felt like I needed to tell him I had started to have issues with my vision in my left eye. To be safe, Dr. Tse referred me to Dr. Albini.

Dr. Albini ordered an EKG for the eye—an electroretinography (ERG). Bromley sat and watched as I leaned into the machine while it created dark, light, and movement patterns to evaluate my left and right eye. Each test, each focus on my left eye, spoke to me, "Be Still and Stay Calm." Though my toe ring was intended for much lighter times of life, I could feel it reminding me to "Be Still and know that I am God" even in the challenging times.

Ever since my first clear diagnosis, Bromley and I looked at the Miami trips as a mini-medical escape. This time, the return to reality included the end of school winter break, work-kickoff events, and transition into a new year.

The transition from Pennsylvania to home had developed its own cadence for the boys—lots of hugs, some rocky moments, and then back into our rhythm. As we neared the anniversary of my cancer diagnosis, several sweet people at church called me a walking miracle. Though I knew they came with the best intentions, they often overwhelmed me. "God, do I reflect a walking miracle?" If they only knew how hard it was to be a good mom and balance life. "God, I need time alone to write and journal."

My reflection spurred me to write a New Year letter to my friends and family.

As many of you know, one year ago, I had my left eye closed for about four months. I never expected to be the one who got the call to come into the office after a biopsy. When they can't give you results over the phone, it's not a good sign. I feel incredibly blessed to have so many dear friends and family to support, love, laugh, and help me and the boys through the journey.

I choose perspective as my great reminder of some of the lessons that hit me last year.

1. ***Don't judge. You never know what someone is going through.*** *I got the funniest stares and sneaky glances at my eye, particularly when it was so black and blue. If Bromley was with me, he got dirty looks. Pretty certain eye cancer wasn't what they were thinking. Those looks became a reminder for me to not assume I know why someone is driving really slow or looks disheveled or frustrated. I have no idea where they are going. Maybe God put them in my path for me to help.*

2. ***No matter what happens to me, I get to choose how I respond.*** *I love that lesson, and it ties to two of my favorite books—*The 7 Habits of Highly Effective People *and* A Man's Search for Meaning.

3. ***It's okay to accept help.*** *I had no choice but to let people help me. In my mind, I would have my eye closed for three weeks, and it would be back open before the boys came home. I had to face the harsh reality that it would be closed for three to four months. I had to have driving lessons again so I could master the one-eye driving, and I had conversations with the boys about why mommy would only have one eye for a while.*

4. ***When you think it couldn't get worse, hold on.*** *I thought taking care of two boys, working, etc., with one eye would be tough. I learned that was nothing when I fell into a boat and fractured a few ribs and bones in my foot. One eye was nothing.*

5. ***I can have both eyes fully functional and still be "blind."*** *The importance of being connected to God and going to Him first when trials hit keeps life in perspective.*

6. ***Parenting is the most important job I have,*** *and it requires constant prayer and guidance for wisdom and patience. Early in the year, Greyson struggled with preschool. I was blessed with a wonderful therapist to encourage me and Greyson. He is doing wonderful in kindergarten and really maturing.*

As January drew to a close and I faced the first anniversary of my cancer diagnosis, I was hesitant to meet with Tim, my counselor and life coach, through the tough seasons. But I'm glad I did. I had met Tim as a marriage counselor, and he transitioned to impact my life much more broadly.

I talked about my disappointment in myself. I accomplished very few things on my list. When I mentioned missing the mission trip, Tim shifted the conversation. "Diana, mission trips are extremely helpful for people who don't appreciate what we have in the US. Those who struggle with gratitude and contentment should definitely go overseas." He continued, "Diana, you have gratitude. You are not blind to the blessings you have." Then, he encouraged me to look for ways to volunteer locally.

Reflection

What a year! My milestone birthday year included an unexpected adventure for me and my boys. So much happened in that twelve-month window. Though my unique imperfections made my struggle obvious during the majority of the year, if all you looked at were Christmas photos from the year before and this year, you would never know. I was reminded that many who look "normal" on the outside have a battle raging within. Keeping up the fight of finding gratitude, blessings, and reasons to laugh was key to my peace. Ignoring the temptation to use an excuse or blame another was freeing; I owned my missteps and learned invaluable lessons.

"You are not blind to your blessings." Writing that and then reading it later in my journal was tremendously impactful to me. I needed Tim's perspective to remind me of the positive growth in my life. I had a tough year, yet I wasn't blind to the blessings around me. "God, help me never to be blind to my blessings."

Take a few minutes to reflect.

- Is there a person you struggle with that may need an extension of grace? Not all battles are visible to the human eye.
- Do you have a focus on what's going wrong that is keeping you from noticing the blessings?

Application

- Make a list of people you struggle with who need grace.

    - ○
    - ○
    - ○
    - ○

- Count your blessings. As the song goes, "Name them one by one."

    - ○
    - ○
    - ○
    - ○
    - ○

CHAPTER ELEVEN

Single Mom with So Much to Balance

One sunny Saturday morning greeted me with many text messages telling me to pick up a newspaper. The News Journal featured an article on the Single Mom's group at White Chapel, and there, front and center, was a full-color picture of me and my boys. It was sweet and humbling. The boys were tickled to be in the newspaper with their mom.

Unfortunately, the joy of being in the paper didn't remove the tough parenting moments as the boys navigated the heavy years. I frequently wrote in my journal, "God, what do my boys remember about these past few years? How can I best help them?"

At dinner one evening, Benny noticed my T-shirt had a pink image of a boxing glove and the caption "Nobody fights alone." How could I explain what it meant to me in words kids understand? I told the boys, "When you're sick, it is important to remember to rely on the people around you to fight with you." I used the example of their little friend, Maggie. Maggie's mom had breast cancer. Her entire family had joined forces to fight with her and for her.

"Do you remember all the people who gave me rides and picked you up from school? I am so thankful for Grandma and Grandpa and Kristine. I'm glad I had them on my side."

Benny chimed in, "Yeah, I remember! And Bromley, too." Greyson added, "Yeah, you didn't have Bromley at the old house." I enjoyed those innocent yet impactful insights into what the boys were observing about my life and the people supporting us.

Although I was one-year post-first-surgery in Miami, I knew I needed to remain diligent to changes in the eye and vision. I also needed to stay focused on my primary Helper throughout the past year.

With Lent right around the corner, I decided to sacrifice sugar in my coffee to help me "Always remember, Never forget." I enjoyed the sweetness, so the coffee didn't taste right; something was missing. It reminded me of life when I charge forward without God in my day and decisions; something is missing.

The company I worked for over 15 years was facing a possible acquisition, making my work days as an executive even more stressful. I had a hard time letting go when I arrived home, but my boys needed 100 percent of me. I booked a three-day vacation for me and the boys at Club Med, my first vacation with just us. I felt blessed to be able to have fun with them without having to cook and clean. They did things that were new and challenging, and I found some time to be alone and reflect. That was the first of many mom-and-boy vacations.

I struggled to balance work pressure with spending time with them on this vacation. I loved it when they asked me to do pajama club at Club Med. Pajama Club was an opportunity for the kids to hang out until 11 p.m. with other kids under supervision. That meant each mom had some time to herself without feeling guilty. This was our first family vacation, and we had a nice balance between fun together and fun apart. I appreciated God giving me a bit of alone time.

Being a single mom, executive, and cancer patient/survivor was a bit intense at times. It took some juggling. There were times when I took work calls while trying to give them a bath or cook dinner. If I could do it over, I would give them my full attention when I was home.

As we neared the end of the school year, I paused to meet with Greyson's teacher to thank her for believing in him. She helped him navigate the year as a good student and a friend. The close of the year was teary for me, as she was an angel I so desperately needed in this season.

The end of the school year also collided with the finalization of the business acquisition. Busier than ever with calls and visits, I strived to balance work with my most important duty as a mom. Within a few months, we embarked on our second vacation to Universal Studios.™ We enjoyed a trip filled with many memories while they learned to have fun together in new environments.

After our vacation, the boys headed to Pennsylvania for summertime with my parents. I started to learn to accept the mixed emotions I felt each time they left. I was torn between the relief of alone time and the incredible loneliness of missing them. It always took a few days to enjoy the silence.

In June, Bromley took me to Miami for another visit with Dr. Tse. He continued to give positive reports indicating no signs of a tumor.

The boys met Kiana when they came back from Pennsylvania. I had prayed and journaled regarding care for the boys, and I ended up searching for a caregiver on Care.com. I never imagined having to find a nanny ten years ago when having children didn't seem to be a possibility. The boys seemed to like her, and they enjoyed their first night with her on July 4th.

For some reason, Benny seemed focused on guns on his fourth birthday. "Guns are not for kids or moms. I don't want anyone to shoot my mommy."

Later, he asked if he was going to die when he was five. "Probably not," I answered. "God still needs you."

"Good," the little man replied. "I don't want to go to heaven without my mommy."

He gave me tremendous insight into how the journey of the past year with my eye and the time away from me impacted my little boys.

As I closed out the summer, I reflected on the areas I could write about when I had time:

- My cancer didn't have a name or a month.
- Pain doesn't have to be visual for people to feel it. Don't judge, love.
- I could be blind someday. I want to always acknowledge the blessing.
- What about divorce? Are we just taking the easy path and not fighting the right battle?

Reflection

- "Nobody Fights Alone" is a great thought on a T-shirt. Many people fight alone because their pain isn't visible. Don't wait until people can see your pain to invite people to your fight.
- I can't do this life over. In retrospect, many times, I put work priorities over my boys or tried to balance both. What message did that send to them? How do you balance your time? What message are you sending?

Application

- Time was an excuse. There is more time than I acknowledge. Are you managing your time, or are you allowing distractions and priorities from others to manage your calendar? What is the best use of your time?

    o
    o
    o

- Review your planner or calendar for the last few months. Below, record the places you spend the most time. Are you spending time in your giftedness? What needs to change?

    o
    o
    o

CHAPTER TWELVE

Five Years Cancer Free... Almost

The world outside my cancer and surgeries didn't move into a "freeze frame." The boys got older, work moved forward, life went on, and finally, I was cancer-free. Unfortunately, being cancer-free didn't mean a return to normal. The multiple surgeries impacted the vision in my left eye.

My medical team at Bascom Palmer expanded to include specialists who could help manage my vision as well as the scar tissue that hindered my eye's movement. By the two-year mark, the procedures started to feel more routine and less scary. I knew I was in good hands.

Even when a suspicious area popped up on my left eye, I trusted Dr. Tse to take care of the biopsy. When most individuals would face stress and high blood pressure, I had the opposite problem—my heart rate and blood pressure dipped, forcing them to pause the surgery a few times to get my heart rate back up before proceeding.

Despite the biopsy being clear, I had some usual medical panics related to the stitches and healing the week after surgery.

Although the Miami team took the lead in my medical care, Dr. Kushner remained my home doctor. He was only a few miles away, and he treated me with care and service similar to the doctor in *Little House on the Prairie*. One Sunday, I texted some photos because my stitches felt loose. Within an hour, he invited me to his house for an impromptu checkup. He kept a medical kit at home, so he was ready to put on his fancy spectacles to view the area up close and use tweezers to fix the problem. His wife took a few photos to share with Dr. Tse, so my main team was up to date. I feel blessed to have had access to a quick resolution without a trip to Miami.

After a few cycles of good news, Bromley and I felt comfortable taking the boys on a spring cruise. I had finally started to trust Bromley enough to move past friendship to dating. The cruise gave us an opportunity to travel together and have separate spaces with our respective children.

This checked off the milestones of the first cruise and first vacation together. Though the boys were young, we created many memories and had multiple "best days ever." It was touching to be there, and feel free to participate in the experience with them. Each day, we encountered new adventures. The highlight of our trip was a catamaran ride out to snorkel off the coast of a rocky island. The captain anchored, and we jumped off the boat. The boys enjoyed the swim to the island and the rough climb.

Back on board, we watched storm clouds form a few miles away. The water funnel that touched down a safe distance from the boat caused amazement all around—no fear, just amazement.

On the final day, I packed our bags but couldn't find my "Be Still" toe ring. I searched all over until I had to put the bags outside the door. Reluctantly, I let go and hoped it had fallen into my bag or the ring would fall into the hands of someone who needed the reminder to "Be Still."

Months later, as I cleaned out my closet, my toe ring mysteriously appeared. I don't think I'll ever know how that ring managed to find its way to the closest floor. It was a humbling reminder that God doesn't leave us and works behind the scenes for our good. I had prayed the ring would be found by someone who needed that humble reminder to "Be Still." The ring found me.

Years Three and Four and Counting

As we closed the summer and prepared for the new school year, I was introduced to Doctor Karp. Dr. Tse asked her to examine the scar tissue that restricted my left eye. It wouldn't rotate properly, creating issues with my peripheral vision. It's hard to describe that experience.

As a basketball player, peripheral vision is key to playing defense, dribbling without looking at the ball, and having a broad view. As an adult, peripheral vision affects driving and parenting. I could see fine when I looked forward. But when I looked to the left, double vision kicked in. It seemed worthwhile to investigate the procedure that might resolve the double vision.

At my first appointment with Dr. Karp, multiple fellows and medical students joined us. She started by briefing them on my story. "This is Diana. She is lucky to be alive. Many with this diagnosis do not make it past five years. Fortunately, we caught her cancer early and removed the tumor quickly."

She spoke like I wasn't sitting in the room. I listened with intent and thankfulness. I was still in the room.

In March of 2017, Dr. Karp removed the scar tissue and used an experimental chemo application as she closed the eye.

The year and a half following the scar tissue removal were lighter with visits and testing. Dr. Karp continued to check on the healing and reduction of double vision in the left eye. And when I saw Dr. Tse for my annual appointment, I was doing so well that he seemed only interested in Bromley's new toe color. Our interactions with Dr. Tse became more personal over the years as we got to know each other. In our early meetings in 2014, Dr. Tse noticed Bromley had his toes painted, and it matched my toenail polish. The color of his toes became a joke at each visit. I was always impressed when he remembered to check out the new color.

Dr. Albini couldn't pinpoint a reason for the vision differences between my eyes and referred me to Dr. Lam. He reviewed my case and requested genetic lab work. However, the lab work was inconclusive. I was reminded that remaining positive and thankful for each moment was still important.

We closed 2018, celebrating four years cancer-free, ready to put the medical appointments behind us. Each day presented new challenges with two growing and very active boys and working as an executive going through an acquisition process. The mirror provided a visual reminder of my eye journey. After so many surgeries, my left eye looked different than my right; the eye didn't open as far, and the eye opening was shaped differently than the right. Many people, particularly those I had not seen in five years, didn't notice a difference.

I was thankful I didn't feel like a cancer patient. I was also incredibly grateful that this four-year cancer journey had introduced me to Bromley. What began as a friendship slowly transitioned. Bromley and I were married in October of 2018. We both preferred a simple wedding, and I'm not sure you could get much simpler than a pastor in our front yard with Greyson, Benjamin, and our dog Bella and cats as witnesses.

Year Five on the Cancer Journey Begins

As I embarked on my third year with the acquiring company, it became more and more evident that the values the new organization hung on the walls and wrote on paper were not lived out by the top executives. Misalignment with values and inconsistency in the treatment of people goes against my core.

A younger version of me may not have said a word. But after all I'd been through, I had no problem sharing my frustration. I have a personal mission to add value and make a positive impact, and I struggled to see that under this new management. The company offered me the opportunity to relocate to Dallas or exit the organization. Because I resist change and worry about how my decisions affect the people around me, this was a tough decision. But I had no desire to uproot my children and leave my medical team.

Prior to exiting the company, I joined the Maxwell Leadership Team with anticipation of a new career journey. For more than ten years, I had been studying the work of John C. Maxwell and leveraging his teachings for personal growth and team development. I planned to take the summer off to reflect and study to prepare for my new role, but I have a hard time being still. Within a few months, I entered my new role in consulting. I would start part-time and then shift to full-time. The position offered a great deal of flexibility. The fact I could work from anywhere was a benefit as well as a challenge.

The week before Thanksgiving, I noticed a lump near my left eye. Since we were heading to Pennsylvania for the holiday, I decided to wait to reach out to Dr. Tse.

The boys and I arrived in Pennsylvania a few days early so I could take my grandmother for her cataract surgery since I could relate to having a doctor poke around the eye. After the procedure, I closed myself in the office at my grandmother's house and called to set up an appointment as soon as we got back to Florida. I didn't realize my grandmother heard me make the call and immediately started praying for me in silence until I shared the news with the family after our Thanksgiving celebration.

After I updated the family, I shifted my focus to make sure each of them was okay. I could see the concern in my parent's eyes, and I didn't want them to think the worst. Yet, in the back of my mind, I couldn't help but think about how each surgery spurred me to visit the attorney and update my will. They also reminded me that many see me as a person with a shorter life span.

I know the reality is that it could be anyone's time at any moment, regardless of cancer. I remember a quote from my days of selling life insurance: "Someone isn't coming home tonight, We just aren't sure who it is." We all need to be ready.

True to the Bascom Palmer spirit and care, Dr. Tse ensured my procedure was scheduled prior to Christmas. Bromley and I both had unique opportunities to connect with fellow patients and their families while waiting for surgery. I spoke with a younger patient in his early twenties across from me in the "medical cubicle farm." Cubicles are frequently used in offices to maximize space, and I could see the similarity with the dividing curtains to create a "medical version" of a cubicle to optimize space.

We talked about what happened and the "why" of his procedure. A dental procedure had gone badly and negatively impacted his vision. The Bascom Palmer team was bringing hope to his future by correcting his eyesight. While I talked to the young man in the holding area, Bromley engaged with his nervous parents in the waiting room. As always, Bromley shared his confidence in the Bascom Palmer team and their care. It was no coincidence that the two of us got to touch the same family in different rooms of the hospital.

Dr. Tse and the surgical team successfully removed a thumb nail-size tumor that they added to Dr. Tse's laboratory for evaluation and testing. I prayed it would help find a cure or a therapy that could shrink this kind of tumor.

A few days before Christmas, Robyn joined me for my follow-up appointment. As was the trend after most surgeries, indications were positive, and margins were clear. I was incredibly thankful and grateful, yet I wanted more assurance.

I asked Dr. Tse's fellow, "Can we do a PET scan?" I wanted to know if this madness was hiding somewhere else. We had gone nearly five years without a recurrence, or had it been there the whole time?

At home that evening, I blew my nose. Never in five years had anyone ever instructed me to avoid blowing my nose after surgery. But I quickly learned what happens if you do. My face looked like a pufferfish. It was incredibly uncomfortable and hard to explain over the phone. I explained to my medical team how it felt and what it looked like the best

I could, and they cleared me to fly to Pennsylvania with my new symptoms.

Our Christmas tradition went off without a hitch, and as usual, while the boys were with my parents, I set aside time to reflect on the past year and set growth goals to prepare me for the next year. Leaving the company I had been with for close to eighteen years topped the list of transitions for the past twelve months. And while I was incredibly thankful for being able to see with both eyes, I felt a bit blinded by what happened next.

Welcome Year Six

Until early March 2020, we felt like we might be back to normal. Dr. Tse delivered great news at the beginning of the year, and I moved back to six-month follow-ups. But I still felt I needed to get a PET scan.

As I prepared for the procedure, I started to understand why many people avoid going to the doctor or getting scans when they have symptoms. Sometimes, the unknown feels easier and more comfortable. My heart prepped for bad news as I remembered the picture of marbles falling that Dr. Tse painted on my first visit. I was incredibly blessed to receive positive news from the PET scan and be able to move on.

In February, I felt the tug to plan a trip I owed the boys. Greyson, in particular, does not forget commitments, and I had promised him we would climb to the crown of the Statue of Liberty. We boarded the plane on March 13 with no idea why so many people were wearing masks. We were still in New York City when Broadway shut down, but fortunately, COVID didn't cancel our Statue of Liberty tour and off-broadway STOMP performance.

The next year and a half, I lived out my passion for adding value and making a positive impact by stepping into a role in the public sector during a time of crisis for Florida and our country. As a leader, I try to never ask my team to do something I'm not willing to do. However, my family worried about me being more susceptible to contracting COVID. So, I made a commitment to my family to get medical clearance before stepping foot on a COVID site.

After my doctors cleared me to serve, I spent many days over the next eighteen months on COVID or vaccination sites, providing calm in the chaos. My team developed the technology solution to manage COVID testing and vaccination sites. The solution was a key factor in company growth during that season. When quoting the technology, we added a line for onsite training, not realizing at the time our team would spend 50 percent of our time on the road at testing or vaccine sites, training the first responders and providing calm and order in the chaos.

For a season, my journey with cancer slipped into the background while I focused on serving in the confusion of the time. Many days, I worked from home with my new interns. Greyson and Ben rotated, sitting beside me in the office to do their schoolwork. We spent extra time together on days I worked at home. If I could go back, I would spend even more time.

My dear friend Kristine came back to Florida during the heat of COVID-19 to care for her momma, Sandra. Sandra was the person who had stepped in to be a light for me at the beginning of my cancer journey, and Kristine sat by my side through many surgeries and tough appointments. It was my turn to sit with her during the toughest season in her life. I didn't know how to help other than just be there to catch her tears and join in her laughter at memories. Sandra was in the last stages of her long fight with cancer.

We honored Sandra before she passed with a COVID version of a reflection service. Sandra and her family sat at the end of the driveway while guests stood across the way, sang songs, and shared memories of her and her impact on their lives. It was a reflective time for me as I cared dearly for my friend. Sandra and her love for me and my family greatly impacted my life.

Reflecting on the lives of those gone before me is impactful. I celebrated Sandra by finding a lesson she taught me that I could replicate when interacting with others. She stepped in to hug me at a time when she knew I needed a friend that understood.

Reflection

My "Be Still" ring was intended to be a motto and reminder for my fortieth year. I think God intended it to be a reminder for my lifetime. I thought I lost it, yet God brought the ring back to me.

- When the lesson starts to fade, how do you keep the most important messages at the forefront and not miss the impact of what you learned?

    Some days, I didn't always enjoy the extra fellows in my eye appointments. Yet, my first visit with Dr. Karp and the multiple fellows caused me to pause. I'm still here at five years, and most patients with my diagnosis wouldn't be sitting in the chair.

- Do you have annoyances that shift to blessings?

    Like any crisis, COVID tests a nation, family, and individuals beyond their comfort zone. If we aren't aware, we lose sight of who we are and what we value most.

- During the COVID crisis, I could have used cancer or "I'm the boss" as an excuse. However, my core values faced incredible conflict because I had to ask my team to be onsite before I was able to lead the way. What excuses do you use to compromise your core values or beliefs because the task is uncomfortable?

COVID was also a time when traditional gatherings were controlled or minimized, sometimes due to regulations and sometimes due to differing opinions that would divide a family or friend group. I will always treasure the unique way we honored Sandra while she was coherent.

- How can you shift from mourning to honoring the person or the loss by how you live?
- Why don't we do more honoring people while they are alive? Why do we wait until someone is gone to praise and thank them?

Application

- Take a minute and think about someone you need to honor. Share how much you appreciate them. List their name and how you plan to communicate with them in the next seven days.
    - o
    - o

- In what area of your life are you feeling conflict with your values and personal mission? Where do you feel the unrest? List the areas of tension and unrest.

    o
    o
    o
    o

- Spend 10 minutes Being Still to listen for guidance on the right next step in each of those areas.

CHAPTER THIRTEEN

Back Again

The vaccine rollout allowed standard medical appointments and procedures to resume. Bromley and I traveled to see Dr. Tse in person for the first time in a year. We drove back home with a sigh of relief because the initial review looked positive. I could return to the routine of serving and helping others by training and providing leadership at vaccine sites around the state.

My next six-month appointment fell in October. I had learned to pay attention to small annoyances and share them with my doctors. I am blessed with a high tolerance for pain and discomfort. But even minimal discomfort is worth referencing. I would have dismissed the bumpy caruncle for years if the urgent care doctor had not said something. The balance of pushing through and raising awareness for the right people became a dance for me to learn.

Post-COVID appointments had a different nuance for everyone. Bromley was not always allowed in the room with me, and masks and screening questions became routine. At my October appointment with Dr. Tse, I mentioned I had some extra sinus pressure and noticed that my left eye was often puffier than the right eye. Concerns related to appearance had become unimportant; however, the appearance might indicate a change in what was underneath. I didn't want to miss a sign of something deeper.

Dr. Tse ordered an MRI to evaluate the sinus area just to be safe. Within minutes of having the results, Dr. Tse called. The MRI indicated that the cancer had traveled from the eye muscle into the left sinus cavity. My head seems so small, yet many experts are needed when the cancer moves to a different area within the head. As I listened to Dr. Tse, I realized the medical team now included an Ear Nose Throat Cancer Doctor, Dr. Weed. He also suggested a prior procedure that had been noted in medical journals—the "Tse Weed" (Seaweed) procedure—that may be relevant to me.

Within days, my cancer care extended from Bascom Palmer to UM Health and the Sylvester Cancer Center. When the cancer was limited to near my left eye, it felt more contained and manageable. This spread to the sinuses felt more unknown and uncertain. In the past six years, I had met many Bascom Palmer doctors focused on vision and scar tissue. For many years, I didn't feel like a cancer patient. But as my medical team grew, I gained perspective on the number of experts needed to fight cancer.

Before I found out about this most recent cancer, I started the journey to be fitted for Invisalign, not for how my teeth looked but to avoid another surgery in the head area. My bottom teeth were crowding, and the dentist either needed to remove a tooth or re-align the teeth. I walked in for my first fitting a couple of weeks before my surgery. The kind dental assistant helped place the retainers on my teeth and then calmly asked me to take them off. But I couldn't move them; they felt so tight, and my fingernails bent, trying to pry them. Normally, tears don't come easily to me, but that moment triggered fear, uncertainty, and frustration.

"I don't think I'm ready for this. I have this surgery in a few weeks, and I have no idea what to expect. Can we defer this?"

The technician was a bit taken aback and suggested I just take the trial pair. I agreed so I could get out of the office. However, I didn't start using the retainers until a few months after surgery. This was a "too much" moment, and I knew I needed space.

The surgery was scheduled for the week of Thanksgiving. I tried desperately to rearrange the surgery so that I could celebrate with my family. I'd been going to Pennsylvania for Thanksgiving at Pap and Gram's house since I was a kid. This was a precious tradition, yet this year, I needed to send the boys on their own and focus on me and my wellness.

The Sunday before the surgery, the boys and I went to church early to serve coffee and donuts. I vividly remember Dr. Kushner calling to check on me while I was there. I sat on the steps and listened to him recap his conversation with Dr. Tse. I admitted to him I didn't want to have this surgery. I was ready to be done. He responded with kindness in his voice, "Diana, you don't have a choice." I knew that, yet it still felt good to state how I was feeling.

Once again, I spent some time with the attorney, updating my will and reviewing changes needed based on my stage of life. As the boys aged and family dynamics changed, it became harder to determine what would be best for my precious boys if I weren't around.

COVID protocols meant I needed to arrive a day early for COVID testing. I was open to any excuse to delay the surgery; however, the COVID test was negative. I had to keep moving because the door was still open.

When Bromley and I checked-in at the UM hospital the next day, I had an hour delay. Finally, the nurse called my name. "Your insurance has not approved your surgery."

I breathed a sigh of relief. "God, maybe this is You. Do you want me to skip this surgery?"

Bromley reminded me this surgery was happening.

We called friends for prayer and got some insurance advocacy, and about fifteen minutes before surgery was scheduled, the insurance approval came through. The UM Health Nurse team quickly prepped me for surgery. I felt a bit unsettled when I learned UM doctors didn't use the purple check mark to ensure the doctor did the operation on the correct eye. The Bascom Palmer purple check mark had become a safety net for me. I stopped them and confirmed that everyone involved was in alignment regarding which eye the procedure was on.

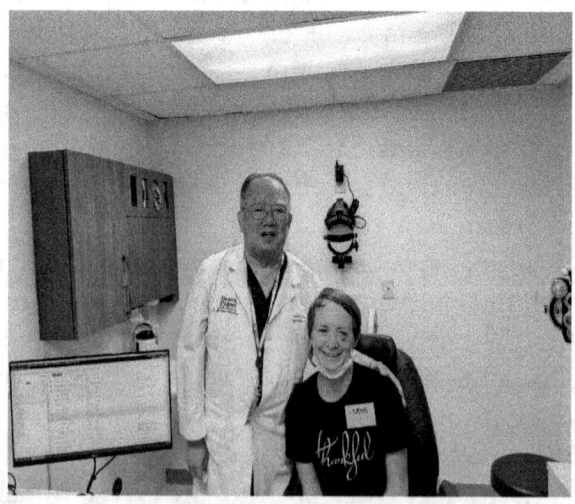

Diana with Dr. David Tse

I woke to news of a successful procedure, a whole new look on my face, and a different hospital experience. Dr. Tse mentioned that my heart rate would dip below forty during surgery. The nurses put me on the watch list and continued to monitor me as my heart rate dipped throughout the day and night.

After one night in the hospital, they gave me the option to go home. I decided I'd like to stay another night. Bromley was in shock. He had witnessed me demanding to be allowed to leave just a few years prior. I might have learned a lesson or two on knowing when to stay.

The following evening, we checked out and stayed at the hotel close to the hospital before heading home on Thanksgiving Day. I had stayed in that hotel many times throughout my COVID-19 test site travels. But this time, I needed Bromley to guide me through the doors, into the elevator, and to the room—all the while looking much like a battered wife.

Our room was on the seventeenth floor, but when we got there, the room key didn't work. I felt exhausted and needed to sit, so I rested on the luggage cart in the hallway while Bromley went to the front desk to reactivate the key.

"Sir, your name isn't on the room." Bromley struggled to keep it together, knowing I was sitting there in the hallway in pain. He explained the situation, and a security guard joined him to meet me in the room so I could verify my identity. A few couples passed me as I waited, but no one paused to offer assistance. It felt like hours passed before Bromley and the security guard arrived, but as soon as the guard was certain Bromley's story lined up, he let us in the room.

This was the most complex surgery to date. I had pain and fatigue I had not experienced prior. Sinus rinses became a part of my daily routine. After all the previous surgeries, I returned to work quickly. I was not mentally prepared for the pain, fatigue, and significant double vision.

My journal notes looked very different this time:

Sometimes, I just want to see with both eyes. God, I'm thankful the surgery went well. I'm alive and healing, and sometimes I can use both eyes and not see double. I've lost my favorite eye patch, and this chaos at home is frustrating.

Be Still.

Help me be still and listen.

I don't always see well with two eyes. Discernment and wisdom were the themes today, and here I am crashing.

Help me see and listen and learn.

As people ask about what's happening with healing and the next steps, I am reminded of a verse I clung to in 2014—"Be Still and know that I am God." Psalms 46:10

The margins tested during surgery indicated the surgery was successful. However, that's what they said before. A team of doctors in Miami and an entire Cancer Board have been reviewing my case and debating on what's next. In early January, we headed back down to Miami to meet with the lead oncologist for his review and insights.

Meanwhile, I strive to be patient as the left side of my face heals. The feeling near my nose and mouth comes back in phases and could take months. The eye muscle is still healing. I have glimpses where I don't see double when I open both eyes. I'm thankful for the glimmers of hope and truly amazed at the Creator. Try covering an eye for a few hours and light a candle or press a button. We are fearfully and wonderfully made. I'm very thankful I can drive on local roads, exercise, and spend time with my family. God is with us!

It's hard to explain the feeling in my face and the tingling. It is a healing journey without an end date. Similar to our faith journey. I went back to yoga tonight after five weeks off. It was *a humbling reminder of the importance of consistency and how quickly our bodies change. When we have the choice, don't give up on the physical.*

The left side of my face was bruised and swollen at a whole new level. As soon as my doctors cleared me to walk, I took off across the Granada Bridge in Ormond Beach and grabbed the fresh air. As always, my need to shade my eye made my appearance interesting. I either wore a patch or used a hat to keep the sun out. I reflected on the many moments in life when I used a million excuses to skip the walk or the exercise while I enjoyed this first stroll. My recovery and the freedom to choose to walk or exercise was so meaningful. It was a blessing to fight for what I could control.

Prior to my surgery, a friend and mentor reached out to offer me the position of President at a company that played a key role in my executive career growth. I greatly admired the couple I worked for as well as the company they had built, so it was a tough decision. Still, I felt this tug to give back to the company that helped me grow professionally.

As I recovered from surgery, I spent many days on the couch napping and listening to a book called *Great Leaders Ask Great Questions*. Many of my answers to the questions that the book posed led me to believe I needed to step away to serve as President.

During my recovery, I truly appreciated friends who called to visit or meet me for lunch. I always warned them that my appearance was a bit rough. But the escape from the routine and the opportunity to see familiar faces was a blessing.

We celebrated Christmas and closed 2021, knowing that January would bring new doctors, more tumor board assessments, and fresh challenges. I fought through to maintain the annual tradition and take the boys to Universal Christmas.

The eye forced a shift from the mom who rides the roller coasters to the mom who holds the stuff while the boys ride. But we were together making memories, and that's what mattered.

Reflection

In 2021, I missed the Thanksgiving tradition I longed for. I'm not sure I even had turkey that year. I wanted to push off or cancel the surgery and looked for doors to close to avoid it. At times, it's easier to ignore the dull ache and sinus changes and focus on others or the fun in life. I could have walked out of the appointment with Dr. Tse and not said a word about my sinuses. I may not be here today, though.

- Are you ignoring nudges or procrastinating doing things you feel strongly you should do?
- What's your response when traditions need to shift?

Application

- Take a look at your to-do list. Which ones are you putting off that need to be handled? Where are excuses getting in the way of fighting for what you need to do for yourself and your health?

    ○
    ○
    ○
    ○
    ○

Uniquely Imperfect, Uniquely Qualified

- As I healed from surgery, I made a difficult decision to switch from a comfortable role that I enjoyed to stretching and serving in a new area. Is there an opportunity you may be uniquely qualified to do and not grasp? Take a minute and think through what you are avoiding, maybe due to a lack of belief. List the item and your next action.

    o
    o
    o
    o

CHAPTER FOURTEEN

New Normal and New Changes

With each round of surgery and healing, looking in the mirror became a bigger reminder of where I started as well as the journey I am currently walking. These powerful reminders remained challenging for me to share with my family and friends. I didn't want to burden them with my doubts and fears. I found myself constantly trying to lighten their loads and present my current situation in such a way those I cared about most wouldn't worry. In my executive role, my goal was to prepare a presentation that answered the questions before they were asked. A similar concept for this medical journey, my goal was to provide enough information to know the next step, minimize questions, and also not scare the crowd.

Despite the strong pull I felt from God to accept the role as President, I struggled to say goodbye to my current team. In my final update to the owners, I shared my feelings about being called into an area that didn't make sense. I loved the ability my position with them gave me to make an impact and provide the greatest value with my skills. I knew I was saying goodbye to comfort and walking into a new leadership opportunity in a troubled culture environment. When I made the shift, I had no idea the personal change and challenges I would encounter.

New Surgeons, New Advice, New Challenges

With every surgery, I held on to the promise this could be the last one. Yet, this current diagnosis had a greater intensity that added experts to my medical team. Dr. Tse introduced Dr. Feun (yes, it sounds like "fun") as my oncologist. Despite his unusual name, the conversations were not necessarily fun. He reminded me there was no proven chemotherapy or radiation scenario to make an impact on sebaceous carcinoma. I learned the importance of collaboration as the tumor board vetted the multiple opinions and solutions. I'm not sure what they talked about behind closed doors; however, I learned to value the great number of brilliant minds and vast experiences reviewing my case on a regular basis.

When Dr. Samuels came on board as a radiation oncologist, I found myself a bit biased against his theory that radiation was the answer. Dr. Samuels was incredibly kind, jovial, and fun, yet I wasn't sold on the radiation approach. The ophthalmologic research and insight compared radiation near my left eye to using a bomb to tear down one house in the neighborhood. Much like a bomb would wipe out the whole neighborhood, radiation on my left eye could destroy my left eye vision and possibly impact my right eye. Dr. Samuels was incredibly kind and patient when I challenged him, and we eventually agreed to disagree. Little did I know I would meet Dr. Samuels again in a few years.

New Normal and New Changes

After our meeting, I started looking for second opinions. My first stop was the Mayo Clinic in Jacksonville. Though I was impressed by the beautiful facility, the doctors there reinforced my loyalty to the medical team in Miami. My window of radiation effectiveness grew shorter each day, so I needed to make a decision. The Mayo Clinic approach would be surgery, radiation, and then, assuming all goes well, no ongoing scans. Obviously, the rarity of my cancer stood out. The Jacksonville team had only addressed a few cases like mine over the years.

Again, I was unique—not in the way I dreamed about as a kid.

The options and the risks the Mayo Clinic presented were pretty consistent with UM. The five treatments of radiation a week for six weeks would take a toll on my body. The treatment would be targeted, yet there were many risks, including:

- If they hit the left optic nerve, it would impact vision in my left eye.
- The radiation could damage my right eye. I did not expect this to be a risk.
- I could have peripheral vision issues with the left eye. Since I had encountered this before, this risk was familiar.
- The radiation could cause possible skin tissue damage. I'm not sure I understood this or asked questions about it.
- It could possibly impact my brain stem. That was a risk I had not anticipated. I assumed modern medicine would be more targeted and less risky.
- With a narrow focus to minimize risk, some of the potentially hidden cancer could be missed.

I had to ask myself, "Will radiation do more harm than help?"

Timing was also a consideration. Doctors recommend radiation take place ten to twelve weeks after surgery. Additionally, navigating a new role that would prove instrumental in my career growth would run parallel to this new cancer journey. In the early years of my cancer journey, I was a part of the Executive Team as Chief Operations Officer and then Chief Administration Officer; it was easier for me to step away with my team's support. In my new role as President, I didn't have the same backup plan.

Constant change and decision-making had become routine for me. No matter how hard I prayed that the cancer would be gone, the adventure continued.

After prayer and more than a few consultations, I elected not to do radiation. Dr. Feun and his team suggested Immunotherapy with Opdivo instead. Dr. Tse and his fellows had been testing this type of treatment in the lab on the tumor they had removed. This technique has proven successful in multiple types of cancer.

Prior to this insurance request for a new form of treatment for a rare disease, I didn't realize the complexity of obtaining insurance approvals for a new medical treatment. The red tape kicks in at the highest level. Of course, the insurance company quickly rejected my Opdivo treatment; it had not been proven effective for sebaceous carcinoma. To me, that felt a bit cyclical. It's a rare form of cancer, how can we prove it works unless they try it on someone first? The Oncology team at UM immediately stepped in to help me write a request to the drug company for hardship funding.

At first, I felt it wasn't worth writing the letter. We had a comfortable family income. That was before I realized that the cost of the drug and treatment would be more than my annual salary. It was humbling to realize I needed help. After a few iterations of the letter, the drug company granted approval with a start date of April 29, 2023.

During the approval process and waiting, I listened to a suggestion from the CEO/owner of my employer to get an additional opinion from MD Anderson Cancer Center in Houston. At some level, I felt like I was "Cheating" on my UM team. I reached out to Dr. Kushner for his advice, and he graciously offered to help me with my "morality quandary." He reminded me that I'm a complex case, and the UM team would be open to anything new that could be learned at MD Anderson. The MD Anderson visit validated the diagnosis and the treatment approach from UM. We left with the agreement to reach out again if the cancer came back after the Immunotherapy treatment.

Prior to the first Immunotherapy appointment, the UM oncology department went over what to expect at the treatment center and the side effects I needed to watch for. I admit it; I Googled the side effects. The long list of possibilities was daunting. The oncology team alleviated my anxiety a bit when I asked what side effects they noticed most often in their patients. The main trends were stomach and gastrointestinal problems, which could be controlled quickly.

This new treatment also meant visiting a new UHealth Center in Deerfield Beach. The thought of monthly IV treatments did not top my list of things to do. I cringe at needles and even pass out at times.

Bromley and I tried once again to make the best of our medical travel adventures. We found some new hotels and restaurants in the area to enjoy the time together the night before the procedure.

My first treatment set the precedence for my new routine. I warned them I might pass out with the blood draw, so an alcohol swab by my nose and constant conversations to distract me became step one each month. After the bloodwork, the treatment started. The first one would last about four hours to allow time to watch my body's reaction. I was thankful not to have a port, so I chose to be grateful for the IV needle. Once the IV was in, I covered that arm with a blanket and listened to my playlist, read a book, or worked. My partner in crime played games on his phone and relaxed in an uncomfortable hospital chair.

After the appointment, we headed home to arrive before the boys were out of school. The car ride usually ended up being a long nap. Though I had just been sitting for hours, the combination of mental fatigue and the need to rest my eyes invited sleep.

I had to trust this treatment to help and resume normal life as a mom, spouse, executive, and volunteer. Thankfully, the treatment was only once a month and life could be normal the rest of the time.

May, June, and July's treatments passed successfully. Bromley and I enjoyed interacting with the nursing team and finding new places to eat and stay.

I was determined not to feel any side effects, so I just kept moving. In late July, I needed a CT scan to check the impact of the treatments. When possible, I went to a local imaging center to avoid traveling to Miami for a 30-minute scan. I had a CD within minutes and shipped it to Miami via UPS as soon as I left the center.

Somehow, the CD got lost at UM. I eventually figured out how to upload the images into my online chart. I didn't lose my sense of passion to avoid the obstacles I could control. I figured out a way to get the images visible to the UM team through the app. The initial view of the images was not positive, and they put my case before the Tumor Board again.

New Normal and New Changes

Intrigued by the process, I asked if I could attend the Tumor Board Meeting. They respectively declined. I then requested Dr. Tse be allowed to sit in as my advocate.

The tumor board didn't like my progress and suggested we modify the treatment. Dr. Feun's note said they would be adding Yervoy in addition to the Opdivo treatment. The two drugs together had the potential to be more effective as well as increase diarrhea. It sounded lovely.

The oncology team helped me with another letter to the drug company, and while we waited for approval, the tumor board suggested I have two biopsies—one from the skin on the outside near the eye and the second from inside the nose. It took me back to my first trips to Miami with biopsies in the same-day procedure room—wide awake and a true test of trust and "Be Still."

The same lovely nurse, Denise, who had been with me nine years ago, was by my side again. It is difficult to describe the odd feeling of watching the big numbing needle come towards your eye, let alone the different smells and sounds one encounters. One biopsy down, and a new treatment was scheduled to begin in about a month.

As I walked this journey, I was frequently reminded of my need to be grateful, ask others to pray for me, and acknowledge my team of encouraging prayer warriors. While I waited for the second biopsy, I wrote a note to my White Chapel Family:

> *White Chapel Family,*
> *Your continued prayers and checking in with me are greatly appreciated. Pastor Michael reminded me this morning there is great hope despite the obstacles. John 14:1 says, "Do not let your hearts be troubled. Trust in God and trust also in me."*

The biopsy from the last week of August indicates that sebaceous carcinoma has returned above my orbital bone/titanium plate. While they evaluate the first biopsy for additional markers, another is scheduled for September 26th from inside the nose (another side of the titanium mesh plate). The University of Miami/Bascom Palmer team is a bit perplexed and is evaluating the next steps. Below is the current recommendation, and I'd appreciate your prayers through the journey. I want to always remember to "take God with me" and "allow Him to guide my steps." Many ask, "Why you?" I often respond, "Why not me? God needs His people interacting with medical staff too; salt and light are needed everywhere." I'm confident God is with me and can shine through me to bring hope to the many people and doctors I've met over the past eight and a half years. Please join our family in praying for the following:

- *God's direction on adding Yervoy to the Opdivo treatment. Current date is Thursday, 9/22.*
- *Nasal biopsy on September 26th. Biopsy will help confirm where the tumor has returned and provide insight for alternative next steps (i.e., radiation, surgery).*
- *Trip to MD Anderson Cancer Center for second opinion on October 11.*
- *Wisdom for the medical staff as we continue to navigate unchartered territories.*

New Normal and New Changes

- *God's will be done, and our family retains hope, peace, and goodness of God in the journey. Bromley and I continue to pray about the balance of information to share with Greyson and Ben.*

As I waited for the next procedure, gratitude for my medical team continued to be a focus. When I met Dr. Tse, I was impressed with his care and knowledge. As I progressed on my journey, I was incredibly thankful to have him in my corner to listen, guide, and mentor me. I reached out to thank him and offered to help him, and he blessed me.

> *Good Morning,*
>
> *I just wanted to reach out and say thank you for your wonderful care for the last eight and a half years! I met you and the Bascom Palmer team right after I turned 40. Time has flown, and I'm thankful every day for you and the team.*
>
> *Bromley is getting a little impatient, waiting for the next steps. Dr. Feun called me three times yesterday with updates. I keep reminding Bromley to be patient.*
>
> *Thanks for your patience with us!*
>
> *If we can ever help you and the team, please let us know.*
>
> *I'm not sure why this cancer likes me so much. Let's figure out how to kick it. :-).*
>
> *Also, thank you for keeping in touch with Dr Kushner. We are having lunch today. Bromley and I would be honored to treat you to lunch someday!*

Dr. Tse sent a note in return, and when I read his words, I reached out to Kristine and Bromley. "I'm not sure why God has me on this journey, yet he continues to bless me with opportunities and people I otherwise would never have met." Dr. Tse's sent these words:

> Hi Diana:
> Thank you for your kind words.
> Your case is very challenging, and we have discussed the best approach to address various issues. I know Dr. Feun contacted you to start the combination of Yervoy/Opdivo on September 22 at DFB, and you are scheduled to undergo a biopsy next week by Dr. Weed. Our aim, as well as yours, is to avoid the exenteration procedure.
> My lab is dedicated to finding a cure for two enigmatic orbital tumors – adenoid cystic carcinoma of the lacrimal gland and sebaceous cell carcinoma. Next time you and Bromley are in town, I would like to show you the lab and share with you the work we do.

On Wednesday, September 21, the oncology office went over the next steps with me and let me know what to expect with the change in drugs. The team was so kind, and I was committed to listen and to fight.

For the first time, I drove solo for my treatment with no issues. The promised stomach issues started to kick in that evening, but Immodium did the trick for the moment.

A few days later, Bromley and I made the trip back to Miami for the biopsy with Dr. Weed inside my nose. As you might imagine, this is not a pleasant procedure, yet I've learned to stay calm and Be Still. The nurse numbed the area via a shot of solution up my nose, and then, after a few minutes, the fun began. I closed my eyes, and Bromley watched the video screen as Dr. Weed magically inserted cameras and needles inside my nose for the biopsy and complimentary cleaning.

To take our minds off the waiting game, we walked across campus to meet Dr. Tse's assistant, Lily, for a tour of the lab. Dr. Tse and his lab team focus on finding a cure for four types of cancer and eye disease. Sebaceous carcinoma is one of them. Lily introduced us to the lab director, and I unintentionally unnerved him by telling him my tumor was in the lab. I shared that I knew my tumor was in the lab because I cared and wanted to support their mission. I think his first thought was HIPPA and privacy, the least of my worries—let's kick this cancer.

It was amazing to see all the efforts being put forth to find cures for the four types of cancer and related side effects. Many patients lose an eye in the process of fighting the cancer/disease. On the lab tour, Dr. Tse talked about his passion for developing a patent for a 3D laser-printed eye to send to kids and adults in poor countries. His idea was inspired by watching a National Geographic show of astronauts in space. Bromley and I left inspired and wishing we had millions to help fund the cause. I also left feeling incredibly grateful to have Dr. Tse on my side.

Back to the Cancer Center

In the middle of October, Bromley and I traveled back to MD Anderson. Though not your average anniversary trip, we continued our tradition of including some fun with our medical trips. This time, we visited my college roommate and her husband, as well as her parents, before heading to the cancer center.

The MD Anderson experience was less than we hoped for. When we arrived, the doors to the waiting room were locked. Apparently, they unlocked on a timer; however, no one knew that, and several patients sat outside the door after the timer did its job.

In the office, the Doctor took us by surprise with her abruptness. "So why are you here? Do you want to transfer your care to me?" I wanted to coach her on communication styles, but instead, I reminded her about our earlier appointment and our plan to come see her again if the cancer came back.

She asked questions about my current treatment and lightly confirmed she agreed. Then she told us, "You'll have to choose which team you want to use for treatment." In my utopian thinking, I imagined both medical facilities working together to find a solution. We quickly realized this wasn't going to happen. I knew the team that truly cared about me was in Miami. We left with the confirmation that UM and Bascom Palmer were "home."

A few days after my visit at MD Anderson, I returned to Deerfield for what would end up being my last immunotherapy treatment. As usual, the staff was kind and caring and helped me navigate the needles and the pricks. Within a day, the headaches and stomach challenges started. But I had firmly decided the symptoms would not keep me from living my life.

Difficult Decisions

God had the timing of my devotionals and quiet time reflection messages firmly in His grasp. The theme was "eyes to see and ears to hear."

- What did I need to see and hear?
- If the right eye sins, cut it out.

New Normal and New Changes

- Eye for an eye, tooth for a tooth.
- God will wipe every tear.
- With a boulder in my eye, don't try to take out the splinter in another's eye. (Matthew 7:1-6)

Possibly, one of my favorite devotional reminders was to act like a survivor until the end.

Dr. Tse called to check in a few days after my last Immunotherapy appointment. Somehow, he knew I went to MD Anderson and asked if they had any additional ideas. I appreciated that he was open to collaboration with other medical teams.

I kept joking about this cancer really liking me. For the rest of October, I attempted to focus on "God, what do you want me to do?" I wrote questions in my journal, waiting for His direction.

Despite the medical appointments, I strived to stay consistent with serving on the board at White Chapel/Warner Christian Academy of South Daytona. On October 25, 2022, I attended the church board meeting. I felt God wanted me to keep the cadence of normal life and not let the cancer control my mind or actions. The elder board prayed for me, and I told them I was asking God, "Do you want my eye?"

That night, I woke up with intense stomach issues. The immodium lost its magic; it didn't help at all! Thanks to God's perfect timing, I had an appointment with Dr. St. James, my family doctor, the next day, and Dr. Fuen's office returned my call while I was in my PCP's office. The two doctors discussed how best to help with the stomach issues. God saw me and orchestrated some amazing timing to help me in this uncomfortable spot.

Uniquely Imperfect, Uniquely Qualified

On November 3, as Florida prepared for Hurricane Nicole, I sent Dr. Feun an agenda to prepare him for our upcoming Zoom meeting. I don't think most patients had his email address, but I was determined to be able to copy more than one doctor on a message. The mission had become extremely urgent.

> *Dr. Feun,*
>
> *My end goal is to live a healthy, fruitful life and be present as long as possible for my boys. I believe I can be healthy with one eye, and I am becoming more uncertain about the impact of the Opdivo/Yervoy treatment on my body. Taking multiple drugs to offset the treatment is a greater concern for me than removing the eye. I want Dr. Tse's opinion on the timing of the eye removal and the impact on my quality and length of life.*
>
> *I also went to MD Anderson for a second opinion at the request/funding of the owner/CEO of my current employer. They didn't have a big difference in opinion. However, they suggested some additional monitoring, including:*
>
> - *Annual chest X-ray*
> - *Annual thyroid ultrasound*
> - *Colonoscopy—some trends show sebaceous spreading there*
> - *Annual skin screens (and then review by an oncologist to determine any trends/correlations)*
> - *Using MRI instead of or with CT to view facial soft tissue*

> At our meeting today, I'd like to review these topics:
>
> - Scheduled scans—Can I switch to having them done locally every time and then overnight the CDs or deliver them?
> - Do we do treatment tomorrow based on recent impacts?
> - I didn't take any prescribed meds yesterday and felt pretty good. Do I need to keep taking them?
>
> Have a blessed day! Diana

A few days later, I sent another email.

> Good Evening, Dr. Tse and Dr. Feun,
> Thank you both for your time, research, and care in trying to figure out the best path for my treatment. Throughout this long journey with sebaceous carcinoma, I have tried to stay healthy and active and be a diligent and loving mother, wife, and employee. I'm not sure I'm always the best patient, but I try. :-) I realize some of our dialogue would be easier if I lived closer. I wanted to share some thoughts on my heart and some ideas for going forward.
> I felt more confident with the Opdivo/Yervoy treatment until the digestive side effects hit me last week. Until then, I had been pretty strong and determined through this. However, diarrhea every hour on Wednesday night with nothing working to stop it caused me to pause. I'm not saying give up on the

treatment, I just want to make sure I'm asking the right questions and sharing the right information with you.

As the mother of two boys, ages ten and fourteen, as well as being a wife, employee, volunteer, daughter, family member, friend, and more, it's important to me to live a healthy life as long as I can. I really want to be there when boys graduate, go to college, get married, etc.

The stomach ick made me reflect:

- *I am extremely thankful for all of Dr. Tse's care for me and that eight and a half years later, I have both eyes. I would appreciate your insight on the best long-term decision for my body, health & wellbeing. I can accept removing the eye. I can be a great pirate.*

- *I would also greatly appreciate the opportunity to talk with you both at the same time.*

- *Will the Opdivo and Yervoy cause long-term stomach issues or other issues with my body? If so, would it make more sense to do an Orbital Exenteration (I think this is the right word) and radiation? Would that provide better odds?*

- *I have my CT's scheduled for Thursday. I will get the results within a couple of hours and can send them via email and update them via UHealth.*

New Normal and New Changes

In the interim, I would appreciate your direction and recommendation on the following:

- *Do you recommend I finish out the Yervoy/Opdivo, even with the stomach issues? Please share why. I can toughen through it.*

- *Do you want me to get weekly blood tests because of stomach issues? If so, please send me an order to get completed at Quest or LabCorp, and I can complete it locally. I live three hours from Deerfield Beach.*

- *Do you want me to keep a log of how I'm feeling throughout this treatment? For example, I take notes in my journal for stomach queasiness (I often feel like I'm seasick in the morning), different eye sensations and puffiness, etc. I'm happy to keep a log and share it with you.*

- *Is there a diet recommended to go along with the treatment to help my body remain healthy and prevent side effects?*

- *How do you want me to handle the report from my skin doctor on the spot on my forehead and back?*

- *When would you like me to schedule the colonoscopy? My family doctor ordered one, and I would appreciate your insight on timing.*

Thank you from the bottom of my heart!

I pivoted from the virtual meeting with Dr. Feun back into work mode and hurricane preparation. I was determined to not let a category one hurricane derail our fourth annual Family Camp in Rome, Georgia. I just wasn't ready to let that time go. When the flooding reached the halfway mark on my tires, I wondered if we would make it out. With Bromley's help, we escaped. At least, that's what it felt like. So many things competed for my time. At some level, I looked at our trip as an escape from the madness of the house, work, and my cancer battle to just be a person.

We've grown very fond of driving on to the Rome Georgia WinShape Campus, getting settled into our cabins, and shifting gears from chaos to just being. At the family camp, I participated with the boys in activities, worship, meals, and devotions. Just before we left, I wrote in my journal, "Thank you, God, for the opportunity to be a mom and a camper." I felt blessed to be able to hang up the hats of cancer patient, executive, and wife for a weekend.

Facing Change

The week before Thanksgiving, I met with Dr. Feun again to review my current situation and next steps. For so many years, I hadn't really felt like a cancer patient, but now, the reality of my challenge began to sink in. I longed for a miracle. Even more, I wanted to walk in God's will and trust He had my hand. I started to process the realization that my eye needed to go. Many times, I'd written the question in my journal, "God, do you want my eye?"

At one point, I sat at lunch with a friend and an executive peer. As I shared updates and the coming reality of removing my eye, he looked at me and asked a reflective question:

"Are you ready to lose an eye? Have you thought about the impact?" I paused; I had considered the impact but not to the level he challenged me.

Change is not natural for any of us. For many, human nature convinces us to hold on to the present as tightly as possible rather than look for ongoing growth and transformation. As an S-personality (Steadiness in DISC), I resist change unless I'm well connected to the end goal and vision. In this case, the alternative to removing the eye was to allow the cancer to keep heading toward my brain. Removing my eye seemed like the best way to be here for my boys and husband. My friend's question evoked tears, and I knew I needed to spend more time with God contemplating the answer in my quiet time.

The prior year, I hadn't made it to Thanksgiving with my family in Pennsylvania. This year, the boys and I went early to help Mom prepare and clean before the rest of the family arrived. After Thanksgiving dinner, I talked with my parents and siblings about my upcoming procedure and the possibilities the doctors were considering. Cancer news, like other health topics, can be tough to deliver. So much feels out of my control. When someone admits to an addiction, they can speak with confidence about their plan to defeat the disease and hold themselves accountable. With cancer, the accountability and prevention steps are a bit vague. I can only act on what I can control—a positive mindset, my relationship with God, and my physical activity and health. I have no control over the outcome.

At times, my mother got frustrated trying to balance cancer with my history of healthy living and exercise. "You are healthy, and you still have cancer. Why should we fight to stay healthy if this happened to you?" My response has stayed consistent. "I don't know why this cancer is with me.

I am confident I would not be able to bear the burden, the medications, or the procedures with a smile if I were not physically, mentally, and spiritually strong. I don't know what I'd be like if I had not invested in my well-being—the areas I could control."

Leaving cousins and family is always sad for the boys, and sometimes, they stay in a funk for a day or so. I didn't have the luxury of feeling melancholy as I quickly got back into the routine of home, work, and the next trip to Miami.

I had started to become a "frequent flier" at my local imaging center. Yet, the doctor requested this round of scans be completed at a UM facility. The Miami team took good care of me as I checked in for the PET scan and MRI. We faced some delays between appointments, but the nurses coordinated to keep everything connected and running smoothly. Someday, I may count the number of scans and MRIs I have had. I can tell you it's a lot. I am ready and willing to give my tips and tricks to those going through it for the first time. Bromley also benefits from the team's calm approach and their coordination of the different delays and appointments.

Dr. Tse fit in time to visit with us after the scans. The tumor hadn't changed much since CT scans the prior month. It was hard to determine what was swelling and what was a tumor. The reality is I am a difficult case—not a difficult patient. (I smile when I think about that.) He spent some time sharing that it might not be possible to do a fake eye implant on my left side due to the nature of the tumor and what will need to be removed. The PET scans continue to show known areas of concern outside the head—"It's all in my head."

God found a way to bring humor into our lives at home despite our medical journey. A few months prior, Bromley found a kitten in our garage and rescued him. Bolt lived under Greyson's dresser until he could trust us. Enamored with our Christmas tree, he climbed the branches to take naps and hide. He seemed to enjoy jumping out at us. God knew we needed uncommon laughter.

Seven days after the MRI and PET scan, Dr. Feun called with a recommendation from the Tumor Board. They cited a few scenarios where chemotherapy helped with sebaceous carcinoma. I listened to Dr. Feun's explanation and reviewed the article he shared. I still wanted to talk with Dr. Tse.

I had learned to be proactive with their time and sent an agenda of topics I wanted to cover. I asked for his opinion about the tumor board scenarios as well as data trends on the size of my tumor and other options or ideas related to my health. I understood a prosthetic eye wasn't likely to work for me. I told him, "I'm not a vain person. What's on the inside is more important than how I look."

Dr. Tse started the call with words that have stayed with me: "Diana, for nine years, we have been fighting for your eye. It's time to shift to fight for your life. The tumor is starting to spread to your brain."

Yikes. I was at work. I had the door locked, so I wouldn't be interrupted. I wanted to focus on what Dr. Tse had to tell me. He spent time reviewing the history and ideas for moving forward. Having cancer in the eyelid was normal; however, having it spread to the sinuses and other areas was not. He explained that just a couple of patients have had success with traditional chemotherapy, and part of my challenge was that the orbit does not have as much blood supply, so the immunotherapy was too diluted by the time it made it to the tumor.

I always appreciated Dr. Tse's approach to learning from past experiences and medical advances. This time was no different. He referenced a prior patient who had a different cancer in a similar area. The medical team had delivered chemotherapy through the artery to directly treat the tumor. He suggested considering this option for me to avoid the dilution. The medical team would determine which artery to use—one from my groin or my arm—and insert a balloon ahead of the chemotherapy so the balloon could be inflated parallel to the eye and the chemo would travel to the tumor and not to the brain. The goal was to shrink the tumor to make surgery easier and leverage the balloon to minimize stroke risk.

That was a lot to process. Dr. Tse kindly offered his cellphone number, so Bromley and I could call him on the weekend. Very few doctors are willing to extend that personal touch of care.

While the boys were at Sunday basketball practice, Bromley and I held hands as we talked with Dr. Tse about the next steps. Dr. Tse went through the risks and opportunities around intra-arterial chemotherapy. We were determined to fight and move forward. The next steps were in my hands. I had to confirm with Dr. Feun that I was willing to try a different solution.

Monday morning, I let Dr. Feun know I'd like to pursue intra-artery chemotherapy. I also asked, "Will it be alright to take the boys to my nephew's wedding in Indiana?" His response was resounding, "Live life, Diana." The boys headed to Minnesota to visit their dad's family after the wedding, which left Bromley and me time to process our questions and what was to come.

Dr. Starke, a neurosurgeon and radiologist, met with us virtually on December 19 to explain the procedure thoroughly. My main question was, "Will I be asleep?" I wasn't sure I could handle being awake while a balloon and a drug traveled up my artery. He smiled and assured me I would be out. Okay. We can do this.

A few days later, I picked up the boys at the airport and headed to Busch Gardens for our theme park Christmas tradition. I teared up when I greeted them at the airport, and as we walked through the park, waves of emotion washed over me countless times. I kept thinking, "What if this is the last time we get to do this together?"

After Busch Gardens, we headed out for our annual walk around Universal together with just the three of us. We arrived back home in time for the Christmas Eve Service. Our family dressed with Christmas cheer to serve dinner prior to the service.

Each year, I grow teary when we start to sing "Silent Night." Until they hit their teens, I sang this song year-round to the boys at night. *Would this be my last Christmas to sing that song?*

As we closed out 2022, I felt blessed to spend time with the boys and Bromley, as well as my family in Pennsylvania. Many Christmas verses and stories took on a different meaning or had a greater impact as the fight against this cancer became more intense, more frequent, and more personal.

Today is available to me and to you.

"Don't fear I am with you. I will hold your right hand." (Isaiah 41:10)

"There was no room for Him in the inn. Do I make room in my heart?" (Luke 2:7)

Reflection

The work version of Diana started to share an agenda prior to every meeting with my medical team. I also was more prepared than ever with a list of questions and the confirmations needed. This cancer liked me, but I didn't want to be a victim. I wanted to fight, ask the right questions, make the best decision, and cherish the time I had. I don't love amusement parks anymore, but I love the time with my boys. The financial cost was not as important as the memory and the investment of time.

- Reading back through this time in my journey brings much emotion and gratitude. Today is available to you and me. Are you making the most of today?

Application

Change is difficult, especially if it's something forced on us. I had to move from a "have to" mindset to a "get to." I couldn't put off the appointment and the questions. I needed to pause and prepare to be a good steward of the time with my doctors, even if I didn't want to know the answers.

- What are you avoiding? Are you facing some medical, physical, or mental challenges? Take ten minutes today and write out all the questions you have and schedule time to review them.

    o
    o
    o
    o

- Make room in your calendar to pause and enjoy God's presence and wisdom. Don't wait for the message of shifting from saving an eye to your life to shifting the focus of your day.

- Review your calendar for the last few weeks. Where did you miss some moments?
- What are the top priorities for you to make memories and spend time with the most important people in your life in the next few weeks?

PART III

Uniquely Imperfect

For nine years, we fought to save my left eye. Even after multiple surgeries, many people didn't even notice the difference between my eyes. I spent time during my early years fussing with my hair and makeup. After the third or fourth surgery, I went the simple route—short hair and no eye makeup. I decided to just be me. That commitment was tested in a whole new way in 2023.

CHAPTER FIFTEEN

New Year, New Challenges

Some may critique my balance of family, faith, and work. I don't measure success by my work status or the size of my paycheck. While much has changed over the past ten years, my life mission remains the same—positively impacting those around me and adding value to everyone. Like most people, my focus has undergone refinement, especially in light of my diagnosis. I had to stay true to my life mission while ensuring my heart was well and healthy in order to best impact others. And by 2023, the faces of those I would impact shifted immensely.

Dealing with Changes

The year started with tough conversations at work as I led the company through rough waters. We saw early retirements, staff reduction, and restructuring among a group of people very comfortable with the status quo. Empathy was put to the test at multiple levels of life.

New Year, New Challenges

The balancing act grew more challenging as I prepared for my procedure on January 16. Family, faith, and work remained my priorities, but throughout the journey, I learned to add my physical and mental health to that list. Medical appointments and a reserved, quiet time had become paramount. When I left those two out, I negatively impacted the other priorities of my life.

My care teams at the University of Miami and Bascom Palmer had spoiled me. I knew the routines and what to expect. However, my next procedure would be at Jackson Memorial, the county hospital in Miami. Dr. Starke had the utmost confidence in the surgery team there, so I accepted that I had to adapt to the change in venue as well as their procedures.

One requirement was a clearance from my family doctor. Dr. St. James has shown up for me in big ways in the last fifteen years. He is one of the most caring, personable family doctors I have met, and the wait times in his office reflect his focus on care and compassion. I learned to come prepared to work while I waited. Even though I couldn't hear what he was saying through the office walls, the timber of his voice through the doors speaks to his caring nature as a doctor and an advocate for his patients.

Dr. St. James reviewed the requests from Jackson Memorial and determined I needed a cardiologist to review my EKG. I was stunned. With less than a week until my procedure—a procedure that had been booked months in advance—I needed to find a heart doctor who would squeeze me in. I was at the healthiest weight in my life, and this seemed odd and off to me. The staff tried to get me an appointment; however, it took reaching out to Dr. Kushner to find one who could clear me in time.

Jackson also wanted another MRI prior to my intra-arterial chemotherapy procedure. Though only a few months had passed since the last one, everything looked worse.

Late in 2022, I signed up to be a guest speaker in Ben's classroom as well as three or four other classes throughout the day. I considered canceling, after all, I had a good excuse. But God gently reminded me how important that day was to my son and his teacher.

As I walked through that day, God showed me even more reasons I needed to be there. Each classroom reminded me of my personal why. I wanted to create an impact. Despite my cancer, I still had the opportunity to encourage and inspire.

My next surprise from Jackson was a required COVID test prior to the procedure. I fit it in just before lunch with Dr. Kushner and his wife, Gayle. I'm still so grateful for their support.

I had many powerful reminders from my quiet time during this season. They emphasize how vital it is to never let anything get in the way of the priority of making time to pause.

- Rely on God's strength to step into the unknown. I think many people resonate with my feelings about change and giving up control. I spent years not feeling quite like a cancer patient because my treatment wasn't traditional. Cancer is scary enough when you think you know what the treatments will be. Then, when non-traditional didn't work, we skipped conventional treatments and jumped to intra-arterial chemo.
- This battle is about my heart, not my eye. My choices reflect the direction of the battle. I wrote many

questions to God in my journal—questions about sharing my story, an idea I had for something I called Caring Bridge, and the broader way He would use this season of my life.

The Power of Prayer and Community

If anyone doubts the power of a church family and prayer, they should have seen the awe-inspiring crowd around me at the altar the Sunday before my first procedure. The boys came forward to stand with me and share in the hugs. Those beautiful people touched my heart and soul. The burly, former Marine gave me a strong hug and encouraged me with, "You are the strongest woman I know." My dear, sweet friend Linda held my shoulders and told me, "You are okay." A few words I wrote in my notes from the message that day became quite telling as I reflected on what happened in the next few months:

"In the end, we will remember not the words of our enemies but the silence of our friends."

On the day of my procedure, I went to work for a few hours in a bit of mind fog. "Am I preparing to be gone for two days, a few weeks, or forever?" I finally told myself, "Diana, this is just a few days of vacation, keep moving."

After years of smooth check-ins at the University of Miami, I was not prepared for the chaos and lack of ownership at Jackson Memorial. I was supposed to arrive the day before my surgery to get settled in; however, after two and a half hours of waiting, I still didn't have a room. The front desk made it clear it was not their fault, and when we returned from dinner, we found the staff playing games on their phones. After years of accountability and ownership training, I got a clear view of what healthcare would look like without it. No one had any plans to find me a place to sleep, so we went back to the hotel. In the midst of our frustration, I recognized the blessing in disguise. I preferred sleeping at the hotel anyway.

The morning of the surgery, check-in went more smoothly. Bromley stayed with me until Dr. Starke came to say hello and review the MRI. He explained that the entry point would depend on what they found when I was under, so I needed to be okay waking up to a surprise.

The procedure went well, but I made the mistake of telling a nurse that the foot the surgical team had used for a camera line was tingly. That sent up a red flag. Thirty minutes later, I had an ultrasound, and finally, after hours of waiting and wishing I hadn't mentioned the tingle, they confirmed that everything on my foot looked fine, and I could go home. The distraction of poor service and lack of accountability at the facility almost made us miss being grateful that I made it through the procedure alive and well.

The successful surgery inspired me to have more bravado and stick up for the people I work with as the tough conversations continued. At the same time, I kept watch for the blurry vision and headaches the medical team had warned me about. And though I experienced a bit of both and some spurts of feeling like I was in a fog, I pushed through to enjoy every day.

God sent many inspirations my way to serve as reminders to be patient and not embrace the pain. I realized He always wanted me to look for the light. I found myself pausing from time to time to ask, "God, what am I missing?" I wanted to see everything He had for me.

I focused on the saying, "When I work, I work. When I pray, God works."

New Year, New Challenges

Despite my physical trials, I strived to serve as a leader and coach to my team. Despite bi-weekly CEO meetings, I sensed something was off. After taking a more forceful approach at one of the sessions, I discovered the company merger I had been hired to facilitate was about to unravel. My shift from a comfortable, inspiring position to a more challenging executive presidential role with a mentor of more than twenty years was unraveling.

I maintained a stoic face as we finished the team Mastermind on Leadershift. The final chapter talked about moving From Career to Calling. How appropriate. Not only was my medical situation not panning out as expected, but the promised career opportunity was crumbling along with the relationship with my long-time mentor. January's end forced me to return to my mantras: Be Still, Trust God, and Do the Right Thing.

February began with life in a fog. I struggled with sleep, waking up in the middle of the night with feelings of failure. I felt like I was letting people at work down. To help my struggling team, I purposefully made time to meet with people or walk with them slowly in the halls. I learned about my blind spots as someone kindly pointed out that while people appreciated meeting with me, some would be more open if I visited their office—their comfort zone. Though it seemed like a small adjustment, it was worth the tweak to better connect and build trust.

It was difficult to do the right thing when I couldn't share all the factors at hand. My heart was in the right place, and I strove to be a light, but not having permission to give full disclosure was a time of testing. One Proverb stood out in this season: "Better to remain silent and be thought a fool than to speak and remove all doubt." Noted.

I did my best to balance my lack of sleep and headaches and kept pushing through the symptoms so I could be there to lead in every aspect of life. I reconnected with my life coach and admitted some days I felt like playing the "cancer card," so I could hide. He commended my loyalty to the people in my life, and he recognized that no matter the situation, I strive to stay true to the people I serve and the commitments I've made. Tears welled up. *Does anyone realize how much I care?*

Devotionals and quiet time prepared me for my toughest season. I didn't expect the tough season to include having to forgive someone who had been dear to me for many years. The devotional in mid-February challenged me to think about prayers not being answered due to unforgiveness. I couldn't think of any grudges I was holding. I spent years watching unforgiveness break apart families and wanted no part. Yet, here I was in the midst of a company falling apart because of pride, lack of communication, and unforgiveness.

Communicating with trust and transparency became more of a challenge as the situation progressed at work. People looked to me to lead. However, despite my title, I was not the one in charge. The undercurrents were strong, and I committed to staying with the company to handle separation agreements and other transition details. While I held true to my end of the commitment, I was also preparing for my next treatment.

The day before my second intra-arterial chemo treatment, we visited Dr. Weed and Dr. Tse. Everything seemed stable, and it looked like I was tolerating the chemo well. Dr. Weed double-checked my appointment with the neurosurgeon. Bromley and I often reflected on the different DISC personalities of the medical team. They balanced the clinical, the processes, and the relationships well.

No need to check in the night before, so we arrived rested and ready for the day. The treatment was delayed for some time because the medicine had some specifications it had to meet. It had to be the right temperature, so the surgical team had to balance the timing of the surgery with the pharmacy and the surgeon. The procedure went smoothly, and I soon found myself back in the hospital room.

Dr. Tse reached out to check on me as we drove home the next day. And I asked the same question I ask after every procedure—"What's next?" It was easier for me to wait patiently when I knew what was coming. My supportive friends and family were not as patient.

Dr. Tse was always curious about how my eyes responded to the treatment. After round two, the left eye was a bit puffier, and the vision blurrier. The pain and discomfort were a little more intense but not a showstopper for me. I knew I would lose the left eye in a few months; this was just a preparation season for the inevitable.

Within a week, I met Dr. Morcos, a well-respected neurosurgeon. People told me neurosurgeons have a "God-like" demeanor. I didn't sense that with Dr. Morcos. He was kind and smiled when he jokingly said he had to go on vacation to prepare for my case. He was also open and honest and answered all my questions. "Diana," he said, "this will be a 'Knock Your Socks Off' moment." I kept wondering what he meant. He clarified by indicating I may not want to leave my house for a few months after the surgery.

Dr. Morcos was pleased that the November and January MRIs looked similar. He agreed with Dr. Weed and Dr. Tse that we would do another MRI in March to ensure that the chemo was shrinking the tumor before the final round of intra-arterial chemo.

As always, I updated Dr. Tse and Dr. Feun about how I was responding to the last treatment and gave them a rundown of the session with Dr. Morcos. My vision in my left eye had become problematic at times with double vision, and the headaches were lasting longer.

As we learned more about the intensity of the surgery and recovery, Bromley decided we needed to say goodbye to our current house. That's always so hard for me. This time, it meant saying goodbye to a house full of memories with the boys—slide parties and sunrises on the front porch. Yet, I knew he was right. This house wasn't well suited for healing. Let's face it: A spiral staircase to the master suite was not a brilliant combination for a patient recovering from head surgery and learning to maneuver life with one eye.

We entered a season of goodbyes. We said farewell to our home (but not the memories), an eye, my role at work, and a person I thought was a dear friend. God inserted his timing and guidance for a new house. The boys and I went to the open house, and we made the offer the same day. The boys immediately claimed their rooms. They were ready to make the change. I struggled with saying goodbye to my dream of tearing down the Beach Street house and rebuilding the perfect home. I found myself frustrated that I had left my prior employer. Finances would have been so different had I still been there. But I had put a tremendous amount of prayer behind the shift. God had a reason, even though I didn't quite understand it yet.

March would be our last chance for fun prior to surgery. I built time in my calendar to make memories with the boys, though Bromley didn't quite understand it. Ben and I went to a Cain concert—what a blessing! Some of their songs led to tears running down my face. I had a mix of strong emotions—gratitude, belief, uncertainty, and confidence.

New Year, New Challenges

It was freeing to take a last-minute trip with the boys to Texas for Spring Break. The boys love amusement parks and roller coasters, and I thought the whirlwind trip would be a great chance to visit my college roommate. I hesitated to ride the roller coasters; however, I did take a chance on the Wonder Woman ride. Wonder Woman and I share a first name as well as a passion to push forward bravely and help others. I don't normally buy souvenirs for myself at parks, but on that day, I thought I needed a Wonder Woman hat to remind me to be strong and push through.

We returned home to the reality of multiple countdowns—the countdown to surgery, the countdown to moving, and the countdown to selling the house. The first two happened just a week apart.

From a work perspective, I shared the news of my surgery and transition from the position of choosing the positive in the April newsletter. Many employees stopped to thank me for the reminder to choose positively and to wish me well.

My last day at work before surgery was odd. *Do I say goodbye to everyone or just slide out the back door, believing I'll be back again?* I slid out the back door.

A few weeks before surgery, I headed in for my last pre-surgery MRI. By now, many on the team recognized me, and I realized that many were praying for a successful MRI for me. My prayer was often, "God, help me to stay calm and not pass out with the IV needle." We need all different angles of prayer to remember to let God lead the way.

As I prepared for the new house closing, the mornings on the porch and walks at sunrise along the river became a bit more sentimental. I stopped one morning in front of our damaged dock to pray and allow the tears to flow.

When we closed on our new house, the Beach Street house hadn't sold yet. So, although we didn't need to rush to get out, we felt a sense of urgency to get settled in the new space before surgery. We didn't hire a moving company. Instead, we moved things by car, truck, and minivan, one load at a time. We left a good bit of furniture and other items at Beach Street so Mom and Dad could stay there when they came down for the surgery. Many times, I asked God why it took so long to sell that house, and then He reminded me of the peace it provided my parents while they helped us during my season of healing.

Every day presented an opportunity to wonder what life would be like after surgery. When I went for my hair appointment, I found myself wondering what it would be like the next time I came in. Little did I know the surgery team would give me a stellar partial head shave.

The Sunday before surgery, Bromley, the boys, my parents, and I all headed to church. I was determined to keep my promise to help serve the coffee and donuts that morning. During those moments of being overwhelmed, shifting to a heart of service has been a key to peace in my life. It helps the worry and the focus shift from me and my problem to: Who can I help, God? Who can I serve? The posture change is irreplaceable and likely kept me from moments of depression and withdrawal.

I will never forget that Sunday as we closed the service with prayer at the altar. Bromley and the boys knelt beside me as a flood of people surrounded us. Prayers and tears flowed all around. We counted this as one of the final game-day preparations.

Calling it a game day may sound odd, but I learned to transition my fear of IVs and surgery to the mindset of game day. We—God, my family, prayer warriors, and surgeons—are all preparing to win this cancer battle. I call it game day because we are determined to win this cancer fight and choose positive.

I had posted this message in the Prayer Group prior to that Sunday morning:

Good Morning, White Chapel Prayer Team,

My updates to the prayer chain allow me to reflect on what I'm learning through this journey. Thank you for reading and praying with my family. As we prepare for Easter, I've been reflecting on Jesus and His journey. Through His suffering, His perspective was on the ultimate result (joy before Him) more than the painful process (Hebrews 12:1-2). It is a reminder for me to focus on Him and allow His peace and strength to guide me through and be a light for Him. This is easier to write than to do.

Last week, I shared my story with my leadership team at work, and it's hard not to be able to answer all the questions: How long will it take to heal? How long will you need to be remote?

Only God knows, and I need to be okay with that. I greatly appreciate your prayers and encouragement for me, Bromley, Greyson, Ben, family, surgeons, and everyone who has surrounded me on this journey.

Many of you have told me that details are helpful as you pray. Lord willing, this is the timeline:

- *April 5 - Check into hospital in Miami for MRI, CTI, and blood work.*
- *April 6th - Surgery. We're looking at 10+ hours with four surgeons (neuro, eye, nose, and plastic surgeon)*
- *About one week in the hospital as the impact to the skull/brain area will "knock my socks off," as the neurosurgeon put it.*
- *Recovery at home for up to 6 weeks. The timeline will be clearer after surgery as they are able to run tests on the tumor and determine if radiation and chemotherapy are a part of the treatment plan.*

I will miss seeing all of you at church on Sundays post-surgery. Look forward to seeing you all at the coffee/donut area tomorrow.

I appreciate you all, and I'll see you Sunday!

Game Day

The countdown to game day became even more intense. The boys still had school, so I maintained a work schedule on Monday and Tuesday. I had one last work meeting with Kristine at Stonewoods on the Tuesday before surgery. I was teary as I talked about all the unknowns and missing Easter with the boys. I shared my work disappointments and blessings as I spent some time with my dearest friend, who had been on this journey with me since the beginning.

After my work meeting with Kristine, I quickly shifted to one last photo shoot with the family and both eyes. Looking back on the photos, you can see the cancer-fighting to take over that left eye.

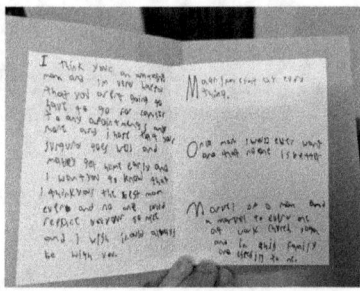
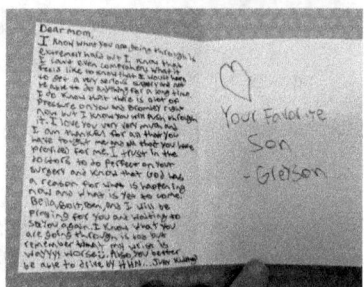

In my daily quiet time, God reminded me to claim His peace. Jesus focused on the ultimate result, not the painful process. I noted in my journal, "I'm not having surgery to remove my eye. I'm having surgery to remove the cancer." Sometimes, we have to lose some good to get rid of the bad.

On Wednesday, Bromley and I headed to Miami. I wasn't sure what lay ahead. I just knew I was stepping away and wouldn't come back looking the same on the outside.

I found comfort in knowing the surgery was at the UM Tower. They cared for me so well in 2021. We checked

Bromley in at the hotel and made sure to add his name to the room to avoid a recurrence of the lesson from 2021. Then we walked over to the Tower and had some coffee while they got my room ready.

As we sipped our coffee, I told Bromley about my idea for Caring Bridge. I'd been praying about it for a few months. I pictured it as a balance between a blog focused on my cancer journey—my progress and the lessons I learned—and a tool for Bromley to use to easily update family and friends.

When the room was finally ready, the nurses kindly welcomed me and started the fun process of IVs and hospital gowns. Bromley and I shared a long hug before he headed to his hotel room. Alone for the evening, I launched Caring Bridge and shared it via Facebook. The new online space prompted phone calls and texts of prayers and best wishes.

The nurses woke me early on April 6, and Bromley arrived soon after to be with me as long as possible. When I was finally transported to the pre-op area, I mentioned that I missed the purple X Bascom Palmer put on my affected eye. "We need to make sure we take out the correct eye." Then, with a mix of smiles and laughs, Dr. Weed stopped in to remind me of the plan for the day.

I'm sure the hours felt like days to my family. I had called the boys prior to surgery since I figured I would not be talking well that evening. Bromley told me later that the surgical team kept him updated throughout the day. As each surgeon finished, they called him with an update. The procedure started with Dr. Morcos going in through my skull to remove the portion of the tumor on the dura, and then Dr. Weed handled the sinus areas. Dr. Tse took out the orbit, and then Dr. Kaye rounded out the relay by using tissue, fat, veins, and arteries from my left leg to fill in the gap on the left side.

I don't know if I'll ever forget the feeling of waking up. I was freezing cold and shaking badly. I just wanted more blankets because I couldn't get warm. I don't remember ever being so cold. In the midst of the shivers, I found gratitude, "God, we made it. I'm alive."

They moved me to intensive care that evening under strict instruction to lay still for twenty-four hours. I don't recall any intense pain, but I'm sure the grogginess came from being drugged pretty well. When Bromley came into the room for the first time, I heard his sniffles and realized I hadn't looked in a mirror yet. The nurses treating me acted like I looked pretty normal, so I didn't realize the impact of my new look until I heard Bromley's tears.

True to his nature, he started to take pictures to share with family and track the recovery process. What alarmed me most was my very crooked smile. While many might have thought I'd have been concerned about my eye, one of my main questions for the doctors was, "Will this smile get better?"

The plug in my nose reminded me of the Angry Birds pigs. My hair … well, let's just say neurosurgeons are not known for quality haircuts. I had multiple monitors and drains hooked up to me. Probably most pronounced for me was the constant thumping noise that reminded me of a baby's heartbeat on an ultrasound. No one had warned me about the "noise monitor."

"What's the thumping in my nose," I asked the doctor.

"Well, Diana, that noise helps us know the skin graft is alive and connected. The connection with the veins and arteries sometimes fails after surgery. The noise means blood is flowing, and the graft is living."

Okay, I can tolerate the noise. It's good news.

After a few days, they moved me from intensive care to a normal floor, and a few days later, physical therapy began. The physical therapy team kindly surrounded me. That was important as I learned to balance walking with one eye and dealt with some pain in my left leg where they had taken grafts.

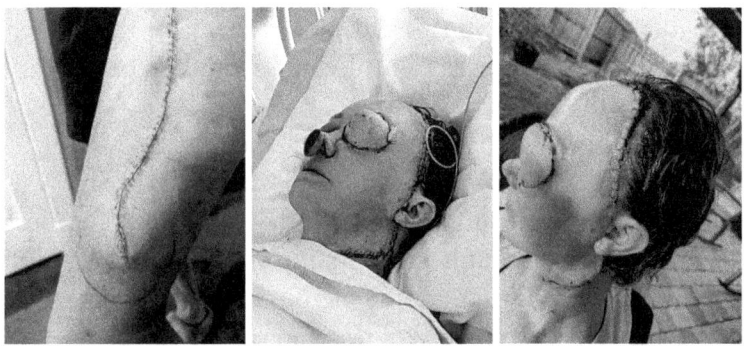

Easter in the hospital was not what I hoped for when the year began. Yet, I realized I was not in a state to attend an Easter service. Mom and Dad took the boys to the sunrise service at SeaWorld, and I listened to the White Chapel service online. I felt very far away.

Mom and Dad wanted to visit and bring the boys, but the wording on the visitation policy wasn't clear. So, we checked with the staff. We got approval, so the boys skipped school on Monday.

When they arrived, patient services told them the boys couldn't come to my room. Bromley tried hard to keep his cool while he reminded them of the conversation less than twenty-four hours prior. Within about thirty minutes, Ben walked in with my mom.

Though Mom and Dad had shown the boys photos to prepare them for my new look, one quick glance and Ben ran out of the room. My twelve-year-old was in tears, shocked by the view of his mom. My own mom was a bit unsettled herself.

"Please go get Ben," I calmly told my mom. "He's scared. Tell him he can just look to the right and stay on my good side." He returned with a quick hug and brief conversation.

Greyson came in with my dad and added his humor to the situation. "Mom, you look like you're ready for Halloween Horror Nights." He was right. I could fit right in as a scary actor.

He definitely lightened the room, and after a few laughs, we changed the subject to his upcoming surgery. He was scheduled for wrist surgery the next day. He decided to "just get it done" even though Mom couldn't be there to take him. We had a nice visit, and after the boys left, Bromley and I walked the hall together. Progress and patience.

On the fifth and sixth day, the medical team took out some of the stitches. I had hundreds in my head, neck, and leg. My boys asked me later, "Did they numb you to remove the stitches?" No, they didn't. I had to just sit still and breathe and pray.

It was a mixture of delight and hesitation when the medical team offered to let me go home one day earlier than expected. I definitely wanted to be in my own bed, but was I ready to handle this without the nurses and medical staff? We would soon find out.

Reflection

As I reflect on the surgery and early healing days, I am incredibly thankful for the early lessons my grandmother taught me about walking with God and seeing the best in each day. The mental toughness lesson from high school basketball mixed in with laughter from Mr. Fox came in handy as well. Remembering to choose positively and owning my response was instrumental in maintaining my mental health and being a comfort to those who came to visit me. It was hard to prepare my boys for what their mom would look like. It was almost as hard to prepare my adult friends for what they would see. I worked to keep smiling through it—even if the smile was crooked.

I started the Caring Bridge to help Bromley and Kristine communicate health updates as well as a channel for me to share my journey with those who cared.

- Are you allowing adversity to block you from blessing others or choosing positivity?
- Where could gratitude play a larger part in your story?

Application

- Think through a moment when your scars were bigger and deeper than expected. What do you need to do to heal from those scars?
- Have you embraced the lessons and possibly created laughter from your moments of adversity? If so, what can you share with others experiencing a similar pain?

CHAPTER SIXTEEN

Back Home, New Look

Bromley drove home at his normal pace. I needed to stop for a bathroom break, and I can only imagine how alarming my appearance was to the Chipotle crew. When we pulled into the driveway, I expected the boys to run out to see me. Ben came out with hesitation and then ran back into the house, still scared by my appearance. It took a few days for him to warm up and realize his mom was going to be okay. Greyson was still foggy from his surgery, so running out to greet me wasn't really an option. Regardless, it was a blessing to be home.

For many years, my husband had been telling me to take time for me and rest. Walker-bound with orders not to drive, I had little choice. I had strict orders to sleep with my head propped up so Bromley wouldn't bump me in bed. For the first few nights, Greyson and I both slept in recliners in the living room. He was recovering from wrist surgery, and I liked the security of sleeping where no one could bump me.

It was about ten days before I was brave enough to sleep in my bed, propped up with pillows.

Home at Last

My first few weeks home, Kristine came to spend each day with me. I napped frequently between talking, reading books, and taking care of work demands.

Earlier in the year, I had been invited to speak on Healthy Conflict at a Church Planters conference. Prior to surgery, I had determined I would still speak via Zoom. I reluctantly admitted I wasn't ready for even a virtual audience. Instead, I wrote a letter for Robin to read to the audience and prayed from afar.

On my first Saturday at home, visitors dropped in all day to give hugs and encouragement. I don't know if anyone knew what to expect. A picture may be worth a thousand words, but I don't think those pictures Bromley took adequately prepared my friends for a face-to-face visit.

Seventeen days after surgery, I was determined to get out of the house. It was time for a dinner date. I tried to cover the hairline scars with a scarf.

We went to one of our favorite small restaurants, Chucherias, and sat in the corner. It was so freeing to be out and away from home. I have always been a slow eater, but the impact to my left jaw slowed me down even more. Bromley ordered the whole fish—bones and all—in hopes we would finish at the same time.

Each day brought new experiences as I navigated my new life. I was allowed to take short walks to build up my strength and endurance. And the surgery left my sight and smell temporarily limited. One night, after applying deodorant several times to conquer what he thought was his body odor, Ben came out to check on the smell in the kitchen. I had inadvertently put my neck wrap in the microwave for too long, which led to a fire. Thankfully, he came out to the kitchen to find the true source of the smell. Laughter is wonderful medicine.

At the end of April, Bromley and I headed to Miami for our first follow-up appointments. I have to admit being so far away with all the stitches and intense recovery felt a bit daunting. As a technology user, I became known for interactions with my medical team through the UHealth app. I sent photos with my chats to bridge the gap and stay connected to my doctors.

The night before my first follow-up appointment, I told Bromley I just wanted to cry. I couldn't get comfortable, and I missed home and normal.

Follow Up

Dr. Morcos' staff removed the rest of the stitches—again without numbing. My efforts to memorize Psalms 23 paid off. The doctor discussed the impact of the surgery. "You'll need to limit yourself to light activity and keep sleeping with your head elevated for at least three more weeks," I asked about my smell and discovered they had also removed the olfactory nerve on my left side. They believed that is how the cancer traveled to the lining of my brain.

At Dr. Weeds' office, we asked about cleaning my nose and the next steps. He had recommended six weeks of radiation; however, traveling to Miami for so many visits sounded disruptive. But when I asked about taking the radiation closer to home, Dr. Weed reminded us how the staff at UHealth truly worked as a team. Within a few minutes, Dr. Samuels came in to tell us how proton radiation would be best for me. When he left the room, Bromley looked at me. "We are coming here for radiation." I wasn't looking forward to six weeks away from home.

I slept most of the way home and then spent some time with the boys. I didn't tell them about the prospect of six weeks away from home. It was still too much for me to process, let alone help them work through it.

I continued to post on Caring Bridge. I found great peace from being open and transparent and hopefully being an inspiration to others.

In the four years I was part of the Maxwell Leadership Team, I had never joined an Accountability Group. But the intensity of the months leading up to the surgery pushed me to grab opportunities. I was hesitant to go on camera for the first call. I warned them first, but my openness led to open dialogue around my journey and what I hoped to accomplish in our ninety days together.

Right after I finished my first follow-up visits, Greyson was due for his stitches to be removed. I tried to give him some of my tips on remaining calm and not passing out, but he was extremely nervous about getting the cast off and stitches out. Before they could get too far, he passed out and had to be moved to the cast room by wheelchair. Eventually, he started to ask the nurse questions and carry on small talk. It took a few minutes, but he finally leveraged the advantage of creating a distraction.

I attempted to balance rest, recovery, motherhood, and phasing into working from home. I was unsure of where God wanted me from a work perspective, yet I knew that I needed to keep my mind active.

Within a few weeks, I tried to work from home. The computer screen and Teams calls led to headaches and different sensations in my right eye. I needed time to adapt and adjust to the healing process.

In early May, I found myself half awake in the middle of the night, wondering why my left eye wouldn't open. Then, as I became fully alert, reality sank in. There is no eye there. It will never open again.

Understanding how to walk with God has been a lifelong journey. I think the impact of the cancer unknowns helped me be more humble in waiting for guidance. My work environment nine years ago was caring and supportive of the cancer journey. But the new dynamics at work were hard for me to balance. As much as I wanted to resist disability leave, prayer helped me realize that's what I needed to do.

Mother's Day fell about a month after surgery. It was my first Sunday back at church, and despite my battered look, I was beyond grateful to have two handsome boys beside me and ready to support me if needed. I was greeted with many hugs and acknowledgments.

It was a blessing to have the boys back home before my 7 weeks away from home for radiation started. Helping with homework felt so much more like an opportunity to spend time with the boys. One night, I was helping Ben with his homework in the kitchen. A candle was burning—sitting off to my left. I sat casually checking his homework and flipping each page. My sense of smell was weak, and I didn't notice that each page flip of the homework was landing in the burning flame. Thankfully, Ben realized the smoke and fire as we stopped the flames. We laughed, and I sent a note to the teacher with a funny note—it wasn't the dog that ate the homework. This was a new one—"My mom burnt my homework." We all seized the opportunity for laughter and being more conscious of Mom's blind spot.

More Opportunities to Stay Calm

Within a few days, it was time for another trip to Miami for more follow-up and a "fitting" for radiation. New terms and experiences have become a part of the adventure. I wasn't sure what "fitting" meant; I just knew it was not optional.

As we arrived at the hotel, my phone rang. "Diana, we have you scheduled shortly, but we will need to cancel. The insurance has not approved your proton radiation yet."

Bromley began to listen more intently as I continued the conversation. "Ma'am, you don't understand. I drove four hours to be here today. What do we need to do to get approval?" It was hard to stay calm. Bromely's frustration with the system mounted.

I called the insurance company, and Bromley called the radiation center again. In the midst of the chaos, the approval came through, and we were clear to start the process.

As the team came to get me, I left Bromley in the waiting room, where he would spend many hours in the coming months.

The team explained the process. I needed to have an MRI, and then they would fit me for the radiation mask. Okay, that sounded simple until I actually started to lie down.

"Wait, I'm not allowed to lay flat on my back. Are you sure this is okay?" I hadn't been flat since April 6. I had learned to ask questions to make sure the entire medical team was on the same page. This team assured me the doctors agreed I could lie down for a short timeframe.

Sigh. Okay, I can do this.

After the MRI, the team started to put a substance on my face to make the mask for radiation. As the substance started to get close to the skin flap over my eye, I asked them to pause again. "Are we sure Dr. Kaye is okay with this stuff being on the skin flap? I don't want it to get infected."

Dr. Samuels came into the room to reassure me that he and Dr. Kaye were working together. They had planned this out, and the skin flap would be fine. Okay, check another new experience off the list.

Back home, in addition to navigating healing, I had many questions for God. Why wasn't the Beach Street house selling? How were we going to make it financially, living on disability insurance with two houses in the Daytona Beach area and paying to live in Miami for seven weeks? And the list goes on.

I grew a bit uneasy when the appointments for radiation treatments didn't show up on my UHealth chart. I wanted to plan and prepare, book hotels, etc. When I called to check on them, Dr. Samuels remained calm and reminded me that the process included analyzing multiple MRIs to build the right protocol. I needed to be patient. He also ordered one more MRI to help with the final protocol and plan.

Following the last MRI, I started to get odd tastes in my mouth. Though they concerned me, my doctors called them normal and part of the unknowns of the healing. I also had some questions about my hairline incision. Thanks to the Uhealth app, I sent pictures to Dr. Morcos, who asked me to head to Miami for an in-person visit.

My friend Robyn kindly volunteered to join me for the trip. I managed to drive as far as her house. My first long highway drive with one eye went well.

In Miami, Dr. Marcos discovered a few stitches that blended with the hairline had been missed. Thankfully, he was able to remove them and treat the infection, so I'd be ready for radiation in a few weeks.

We also hand-delivered the MRI CD to Dr. Samuels and snuck in a visit with Dr. Tse. Robyn enjoyed seeing firsthand the kindness of the medical team and their care.

As I allowed myself to accept the fact I'd be away from home for not just six weeks but now seven weeks for radiation, I reached out to Dr. Tse to see if he had any ideas on how I could serve each day after my treatments. I was sure I would be bored out of my mind. He gently thanked me for my servant mindset and asked me to focus on taking care of myself.

In mid-May, Dr. Tse called. "Diana, I have a patient in my office who has a different type of cancer but needs to undergo the same procedure with Dr. Weed, Dr. Morcos, and me. Would you talk with him?"

Absolutely. Thank you, God. Help me to find purpose in this.

I talked with "John" one evening. His story included complexities that were a bit different than mine, including past history and family support. He didn't want the medical team to fully remove the cancer. Instead, he wanted to set limits for the surgeon. I listened intently as he talked. Then, he asked how I was able to trust the medical team.

I shared my story and how I built trust with the medical team. I told "John" I was incredibly thankful for them and the trust and relationships we had built with the team over the past eight years. A month after surgery, I couldn't relate to asking the doctors to leave some of the cancer behind. I never wanted to have another surgery involving my skull again, but I trusted the surgeons to use their skill and best judgment.

I felt blessed to be able to help "John" move forward. I had no one to ask about surgery when I went through the process. I was happy to use my adversity to help him.

The week prior to radiation starting, Dr. Samuels called to let me know the treatments had been deferred until after Memorial Day. The updated MRI revealed they needed more time. I breathed a sigh of relief. I would enjoy more time with my family and the boys.

I seized the opportunity to share in church the Sunday before I left for radiation. I told my friends, "God is still good, and His goodness continues to shine in tough times." It's vital to believe this. Saying it in front of a group of prayer warriors helped reinforce my belief.

Reflection

I had many years of practice staying calm as I walked through the unknowns. My grandmother taught me many lessons on choosing laughter even in tough times. The mental toughness lessons from high school basketball and memorized scripture from my childhood helped immensely as I navigated the uncertainty. The thought of being away from home for radiation without a work distraction troubled me. I went back to a life lesson from my youth: Look for ways to serve and help others along a similar pathway.

- What do you do, or need to do, to remind yourself to stay calm when uncertainty brings anxiety? Do you have a favorite scripture you turn to?
- What interests or gifts could you use to serve others? What volunteer organizations intrigue you?

Application

- Memorize Psalm 23 or another calming scripture so you're ready when trouble comes your way.
- Explore places that could use your gifts or interests. Begin serving even before trials come so those distractions are in place when you need them.

CHAPTER SEVENTEEN

Seven Weeks Away from Home

Memorial Day that year kicked off a series of firsts. I took my first solo trip to South Florida with one eye, and I had my first proton radiation treatment. However, those were just the ones I knew about before I left home.

I took my time driving south, especially on I-95. I had rented a timeshare in Fort Lauderdale for this week, about forty-five minutes north of Miami. On my way in, the concierge started to tell me about all the onsite activities and promotions. I smiled and said, "I am here for medical treatment. I don't think much fun will be included."

Week One of My New Adventure

The next day, I took time in the morning to enjoy my coffee and headed to Miami for my afternoon appointment. With all the traffic on my commute, I decided radiation would be easy. However, after I reached UHealth, I discovered I had one more new challenge to meet.

I had never had to find a spot in a dark, winding parking garage with one eye. It's difficult to describe how daunting that task was to someone with sight in both eyes. The ticket kiosk sat on a tight curve. I didn't even get close, so I put the car in park and opened the door to retrieve my ticket.

Like most hospitals, afternoon parking was limited—perhaps more limited than my vision. As I drove up the narrow winding ramp, I prayed God wouldn't let me hit anything. And I couldn't help thinking I had to make it back down later. I managed to park without hitting anything and headed into the hospital to check in.

By the end of seven weeks, the welcome team at Tower West and Tower North would become familiar faces on this leg of the journey. Today, however, I provided my ID and waited for a badge to print before they could guide me to the radiation center. The man who greeted me with his kind, jovial smile was Roger. He got me checked in for my first session.

I only had to wait a few minutes to be called into the second waiting area. The friendly team greeted me and helped me navigate what would soon become a very familiar routine.

As I walked into the Proton Radiation room for the first time, I felt like I was being launched into space. Before I lay down, I asked the technician to take a photo of me with the machine to share with the boys and Bromley. And then, it was time for session one to begin.

They brought the promised mask—that one that caused me so much stress the day they fitted me—out of a closet. It had my name on with markings around the left eye and entry points for the radiation.

"Put your feet here, make sure your head is tight to the top, hold your breath, and lay still as we snap you in."

They got me situated, but it felt very tight.

"Can you breathe?"

Well, yes, I could breathe.

After I started to inhale and exhale calmly, I discovered the straps started to loosen. That would lessen the anxiety a bit. Psalm 23 once again became a cherished prayer as I repeated it over and over for twenty minutes. "Be Still" was the verse God laid on my heart nine years ago. The irony of the inverse wasn't lost on me. "I'm still God. I'm not moving anytime soon."

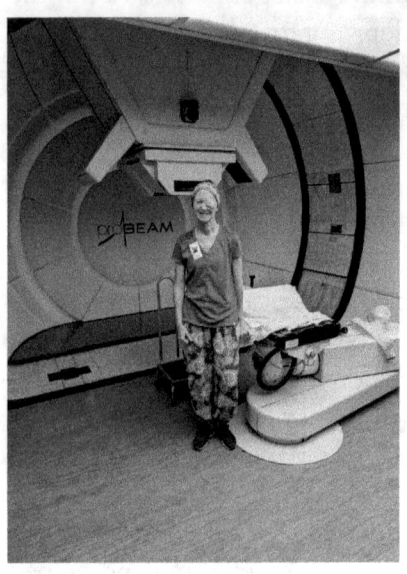

As I headed for the car, I thought, "One session down. Thirty-two more to go." Now, I just had to make it out of the parking garage and back to Fort Lauderdale. One step at a time.

Week one was full of new sensations and a lack of routine. The team set up my schedule so my first session every week would be in the afternoon, and my last session of the week would fall in the early morning so I could maximize my time at home. I felt a huge feeling of accomplishment as I drove home after week one. I did it. No. God, we did it.

Serving at church is one of my passions, and I wasn't willing to let it go simply because I was having radiation. I find so much blessing in serving and helping others, and I didn't want to give that up on the weekends in between radiation. It was refreshing to be at the coffee bar on Sunday and greet and serve my church family.

Embracing the Adventure

As I headed into week two, the redness started to kick in. Each patient responds differently. And my pale skin—which doesn't like the sun—was protesting intense radiation. My dear friend Kristine joined me for this second week.

I enjoyed the transition from a week of feeling a bit alone to a "radiation vacation." I quickly established a routine for the week. I would rise early, enjoy my coffee, and then take a Lyft to the treatment center. My health insurance provided Lyft passes within certain hours, and I was blessed to use them and escape the parking garage madness.

After treatment, I headed back to our Doral hotel, where I exercised and then rested. While Kristine worked, I focused on Maxwell training and my speech submissions. Earlier, I mentioned joining a Maxwell Accountability group for the first time during this season. I also stopped putting off writing a three-minute story for submission at the Maxwell Leadership events that took place each year in March and August. I had time and a unique appearance. Why not submit my cancer thriver story for critique and eventual submission for stage time in front of a few thousand at the August 2023 Maxwell Leadership Event?

Kristine joined me for doctor's appointments during week two. Like Bromley, she came up with questions for things I took for granted. She asked about the redness and if it was normal. Dr. Samuels and his team were always so pleasant and kind—ready for any questions.

Kristine also helped me finalize plans for the Air BnB I wanted to book for the last month of radiation. I looked for a place within walking distance of UM where I could feel safe and walk to the hospital without fear. God came through with the place and the funding. Was it home? No. Would it work for four weeks? Yes.

Kristine headed out Thursday evening after a late lunch. I was sad to see her go as we enjoyed many dinners out and "soul sister bonding" that week. I anticipated my first double treatment day, but the proton radiation team called to say the machine was down. I was relieved for a couple of reasons. First, my skin was already rosy. And second, I had another treatment scheduled for the next morning. Additionally, this second treatment for the day was planned for the evening, and I wasn't looking forward to radiation and navigating traffic while the sun was going down. Friday morning, the machine was ready for me, and then I drove home to visit with the boys on their last day of school.

Week Three was one of my favorite weeks. I know it sounds strange to have a favorite week of radiation. But this time, Mom and the boys joined me on the journey. I'm not sure they realized they signed up for a 6 a.m. departure time when they volunteered to go with me.

Mom and Greyson slept in the car, and Ben accompanied me to my first appointment. The parking garage wasn't as scary the second time, plus I had a support crew. The hospital amazed Ben as we walked through to meet the proton radiation team. He asked to see the machine, and they proudly took him into the room and told him how they took care of his mom. After I finished, the four of us explored Miami.

Ben went with me to my treatments on most days that week. He liked meeting the doctors. Dr. Samuels's team showed him the photos of my head and the targets for the proton radiation. The team assured Ben that the team, as well as the equipment, were focused on the correct part of my head and not my brain.

I was especially blessed when Ben and I visited Dr. Morcos, my neurosurgeon. I knew Ben had a lot of questions for him. Ben patiently waited while Dr. Morcos checked my incisions and asked about radiation. After his team did assessments on mobility and reactions, Ben started with his list of questions. "My mom has stitches on top of her head and all down the side of her neck. Did you just pull off her whole face skin to do the surgery?"

Dr. Morcos responded with great care and respect for the question. "That's a great question. That would have looked pretty bad. We actually made two separate incisions based on the timing of the procedure. I'm not going to tell you your mom looked good during surgery, but she looks good now, right?" Ben was satisfied with the answer, and we were able to move on to schedule the next follow-up appointment.

We tried to do something fun for the boys each day and mix in practice for my three-minute story submission for Stage Time. I also met with a nutritionist who focused on brain cancer and the adjustments I needed to make while I was having radiation. I thought I ate pretty well until I logged my food for a week. The list gently reminded me I needed to rebalance. She recommended a morning prep Keto Drink before radiation each day. The flavor wasn't great, but her advice helped me prepare for game day and create a mindset to fight for my mind, my brain, and my life.

After my Friday treatment, Dr. Tse offered to provide Ben with a tour of the lab. You'll remember that Bromley and I had taken the tour, but Ben got the gold carpet treatment. Dr. Tse explained the four types of cancer/disease they were researching and showed him the equipment. It all amazed Ben. He loved looking at the cancer cells in action and exploring each area of the room. We closed the session by walking into a classroom, and Dr. Tse's team asked Ben if he could see himself there someday. Ben paused for a few more questions before committing. But as we were leaving, Dr. Tse asked Ben what he would like to do someday. Ben responded, "I'd like to find a cure for blindness."

I was reminded of the importance of bringing my boys on this journey with me. They wanted to know what was going on. The fear of what's happening to mom is not as scary when you meet the medical team and see the care in action.

As we headed home after the Friday treatment, we stopped at The Diner, a restaurant Bromley and I had made a routine stop on our journeys to Miami. Georgios waited on us, and I was reminded again of my unique appearance and the opportunity to stand out and make a positive difference in a crowded restaurant. With my memorable look, the staff easily recognized me and greeted us with a warm welcome. The boys picked up on the hospitality, and it became a teaching opportunity.

The next time I left for Miami, the boys headed to Pennsylvania with my parents. Only four weeks of radiation left. Only four weeks without seeing my boys.

The Halfway Mark

Week four was another girls' week. I accomplished another first by driving all the way to Miami to the AirBnB. I spent the first night by myself trying to figure out the nuances of the house.

On Monday, before Kristine arrived, I walked to radiation. I felt freedom each morning as I sipped my coffee, enjoyed my quiet time, and then walked to the West Tower. My route took me past the UM gym each day. It took a bit of courage, but I finally went in and asked about joining.

I soon had a new routine. I walked to radiation, worked out, had a smoothie or Jimmy Johns, and then walked back to the house for a nap. Kristine and I managed to dine out each night and found some new favorites in Miami.

When Kristine headed out on Friday, we said goodbye for a season. We didn't know for sure how long it would be before I saw her again.

Bromley and Bella, our sweet and cantankerous Chihuahua, joined me for the last three weeks. No more drives north solo on the weekends. I could rest and relax with my husband behind the wheel.

With three weeks left, I started to have more odd tastes and some mouth sores. The radiation oncology team introduced me to Magic Mouthwash. I'm not sure what was Magical about it. It was another item to add to my routine, and the taste was far from magical.

During this season of minimal work and a focus on personal growth, I also enrolled in the Equip Beyond Success program. The first time I joined the Zoom meeting, I forgot to prep the facilitator for my appearance. He was caught off guard and thought maybe the camera was "cutting me off." He ended up becoming a great encouragement for me as he reminded me what it meant to push forward as a cancer thriver.

Spouses may feel lost when their loved ones go through radiation. If you don't know what to do, I suggest following Bromley's lead. He spent his time lightening my load and being with me. He prepared my morning coffee and prepped my daily routine. He got my morning coffee, Keto Brain drink, and saline rinse ready before we headed to the UHealth West Tower. We walked together to UM, and Bromley waited while I had my treatment. He enjoyed the conversation with the staff members and other patients in the lobby. Roger, the Patient Experience Specialist I befriended on my first day of radiation, became a friend of Bromley's, too. Bromley made sure to ask everyone his favorite question, "How long does it take you to get to work?" With all the traffic in Miami, he was always intrigued to know the length of their trip and what tricks they had to avoid the traffic.

Uniquely Imperfect, Uniquely Qualified

As we got closer to Ring the Bell Day, I asked God for clarity on what to give the beautiful souls who took me through my treatments each day. A friend designed an image for me based on my values and focus areas, and I planned to write a note in sticker format to accompany the image. I just needed a sweet treat to accompany it. After many calls and inquiries, I found the perfect gift.

We used the Fourth of July to sleep in and have some fun with Top Golf and dinner out, and later that week, on the eve of my final treatment, we prepared the cookie boxes. We arranged the various flavors and added a note and a sticker to each gift.

That final morning, everyone from valet to security to check-in received my thank you note, sticker, and a treat. The morning medical team asked if I wanted to ring the bell, but I had an afternoon treatment scheduled. I would ring it then.

After my morning radiation session, we stopped at the pharmacy to give out cookies and then headed for one more workout before nap time and lunch. We also discussed spending one more night in Miami. Bromley thought I might need to rest, but I was ready to claim victory and go home.

I was a bit teary walking back in for that last session. The routine had become familiar, and the faces represented friends and family away from home. Within twenty minutes of that last strap down, the season was over. I gladly claimed my radiation mask as a new sign of victory and progress. The mask sits on my dresser today as a reminder of the battle.

Dr. Tse and Bromley were waiting when I walked out of the proton radiation room. Yes, Dr. Tse, my servant leader doctor, made time on a Friday afternoon to ring the bell with me. I had walked by that bell for seven weeks. At first, it felt like I would never be able to make it sound. Then, as the number of treatments left dwindled into the single digits, excitement started to build.

I rang the bell over and over and stood for photos with Bromley, Dr. Tse, and my support team. We shared tears of victory, relief, and sad goodbyes.

As I reflect on ringing the bell, I remember the excitement mixed with the wonder if we had really achieved victory. It would be a few months before we would know the score. Still, the bell marked a major milestone. We made it through seven weeks away from home. My face was red and puffy as we walked out the door for the last time, but the smile and tears were filled with victory. We were headed home for the next chapter.

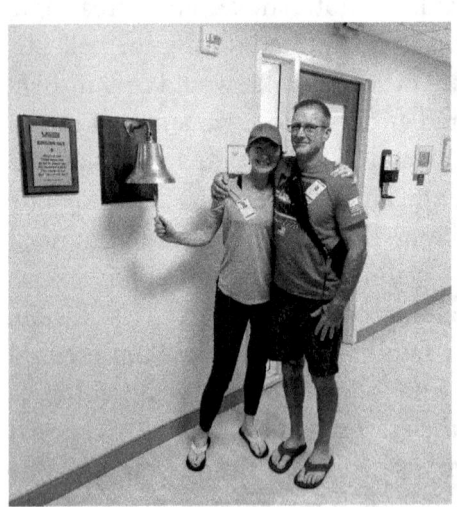
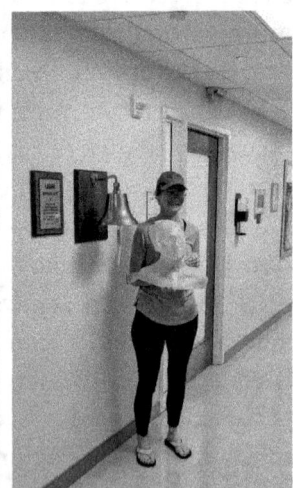

Reflection

Some days, I look back at those weeks of radiation and miss the simple routine and narrow focus—wake up, enjoy coffee and quiet time, walk to radiation, get treatment, walk to workout, rest, eat, and study. Many asked if I used the time to binge-watch TV. I don't think I even turned it on. I enjoyed the time to work on myself medically, physically, intellectually, and spiritually.

If radiation had been close to home, I would have clung to my typical "I got this" nature. I would have missed time with precious friends and family along the journey.

I opened my heart at a different level to ask people to join me. I seized opportunities to impact the people I saw every day and humbled myself enough to ask for help. I would have also missed Dr. Tse being with me for my "ring the bell" moment.

- Where are you feeling the tug to pause and realign what's most important?
- Do you need a medical retreat to refocus your time?

Application

- It's time to grow. Where do you find yourself stuck? What keeps you from smiling?
- Not everyone reading this book has cancer. However, we all have medical appointments or other places to be that seem less pleasant than others. What can you do to shift your mindset as you walk through the door? How can you be a blessing to those who serve you in those difficult situations?
- Where do you have the opportunity to step in and serve someone struggling with an illness? They may

not ask for help. They may be waiting for someone to rescue them from the simple things of life.

Rescue could mean:

- Dinner out
- Taking care of chores or errands
- Lightening the load
- Making them feel like they look like a rock star when they don't
- Laughter

CHAPTER EIGHTEEN

Why Not Now? This Unique Look Makes Me Memorable.

How do I describe being home but not quite being the same? I had stepped away for seven weeks to live a routine focused on my health and treatment. With no one to care for but me, the routine was simple, and my daily engagement with people was pretty routine. I was incredibly thankful to be home and figure out what this new phase of life would be like.

The boys were home for a week with me, attending Passion Camp as I got back into my routine. Passion Camp is a national camp for teens hosted by the Passion Church in Daytona Beach, only a few miles away. This allowed me time to see them in the morning before they headed off to camp and then time to rest during the day. They would then be heading to their overnight WinShape camp in Rome, Georgia. I humbly realized that the post-radiation symptoms were real and felt a bit different in the midst of being home. Sleep was not quite the same. Intermittent headaches and fatigue stepped in, leading to naps and extra rest. As my skin flap recovered from radiation, the peeling and the redness took on a new look and feel. Yes, feel. As the nerves started to recover, odd sensations shot through the area, accompanied by numbness and tingling. The taste in my mouth was difficult to describe—after all, no one can taste this sweet, odd feeling in my mouth.

Gratitude often flooded my heart as I settled in and took in how much the boys had changed and matured in the month we were apart. I started to use the computer more, causing my right eye to feel the fatigue of doing the work of two eyes.

My pride wanted to push and return to work and to normal. So, the need to rest and recover humbled me. Short-term disability made sense. For years, the boys and I had made the trip to Winshape camps a leisurely event. We always stayed at a hotel on the way and enjoyed the time together.

This year, my dad drove to a new camp location. The boys had decided at the close of camp in 2022 that they wanted to try the two-week boys camp at Mt. Berry in Rome, GA. I was excited for them as the Winshape organization founded by S. Truett Cathy in 1985 originally started at Mt. Berry. The WinShape camp experience had become non-negotiable in our summers as the experience, and the counselor provided such a great development experience for my boys. Although I was incredibly thankful to ride with the boys, it was different not being just us. The new location wasn't the only change in our drop-off routine. Dad was determined to save gas, so he turned off the car at each drop-off spot, leaving us to swelter in the heat. I had to relinquish control. It wasn't my car, and I didn't get to have my way this camp drop-off.

This was a bit humbling for me as I had become accustomed to being solo to drop them off for multiple years.

After we got the boys settled, Dad took me to the Atlanta airport to fly back to Daytona to meet Bromley. Navigating new places with one eye is a challenge, and the Atlanta airport was a greater challenge than I anticipated. I normally just navigate quickly through the crowd. This time, I needed to pause and gauge my surroundings to find the pace before I stepped into the crowd.

I had time to eat before my flight and stepped into my favorite restaurant. The restaurant was busy, and my normal bar spot was not open. A kind lady offered to share a table with me. Pause. *God, am I ready to share a table and have an open dialogue about my unique look with a random person*? I did it, and we had a lovely conversation about life and grasping the moments.

Another Month of Firsts

July was a month of firsts at home as I tried to return to the familiar. Without my "bucket hat" cover, I walked into my first hot yoga class after months off. As normal, when I entered a room, I was met with a few stares and then hugs after people recognized me. The up-and-down movements and a few headaches made it a bit challenging. I just wanted to make it to the final quiet time at the end to recover, and I couldn't wait to get home to hold Bromley's hand. It was a sign I made it through another first.

In the last few weeks of radiation, I was impressed that a part of my left eyebrow still hung in there. Dr. Samuels warned me I would likely lose my left eyebrow and possibly my right eye.

Comically, what I thought was my eyebrow turned out to be some sticky matter I was afraid to really clean off. It turns out that I hadn't had eyebrows for a few months.

In late July, Ben joined me for a Miami check-in with Dr. Weed. I told my son that Dr. Weed would use a camera to explore the inside of my nose and possibly clean it out. I let him know it was okay to turn away.

Ben stayed in the corner while they cleaned my nose and came back to the main area as Dr. Weed provided the assuring results from my MRI and nose review. He also told me the tightness in my jaw would stay with me for a lifetime. "You will need to stretch your jaw every day, Diana." Okay, not something I thought about doing, but it would be easy enough.

Ben and I left Dr. Weed's office to meet with the patient experience team. I was committed to sharing my positive experience and serving on the patient advisory board. We met in a cafeteria I had never been to in my nine years on the campus. Ben entered the conversation and had some valuable insight for the patient experience team. This proud mom beamed as my twelve-year-old was willing to engage and give ideas in an unfamiliar setting.

The season of firsts in my new normal continued. I practiced my International Maxwell Conference Stage Time submission often. The conference pulls 3,000+ in-person attendees as well as virtual attendees for multiple days of focused speakers and sessions on personal growth and leadership.

The week I hit forty-nine, I was accepted to the semifinals, where I would present via a live conference call. On the Sunday of the semifinals, I returned home from church and set up my office for my Zoom call with a fake microphone, and I blocked off the room. I would be presenting in front of the others, competing for one of ten spots.

I committed to do my best—that's what I could control. Thankful when I completed my turn, I stepped off the call with confidence as many of my peers sent notes in the chat about my impactful story. *God, thank You. I used my unique look and story to impact lives.*

I felt honored to be selected as one of the Stage Time presenters, and as I prepared, a LinkedIn advertisement for a Book in a Weekend training hit my radar. Curious, I submitted my book idea and jumped at the opportunity for a Zoom call with Tim Elmore. Even if I didn't make the cut for Book in a Weekend, I knew I would benefit from thirty minutes with Tim. Tim confirmed that my story and first pitch fit well with the program concept. I just needed to decide if I was ready.

At the International Maxwell Conference

Heading to IMC with my new look added another first to my season. I had navigated the World Marriott multiple times. The first time, the volume of friendly people overwhelmed me a bit, but this time, I had a new look. I had learned to maintain my confident smile and focus on making others feel comfortable about my new look.

Admittedly, I was a bit distracted on the first day of the conference as I wanted to check Stage Time off the list. I didn't share that I was a Stage Time participant in my breakout group. I preferred to stay under the radar. As I walked to my hotel room to practice, I passed Tim Elmore, and he easily recognized me. A smile flooded my face. I obviously don't love the experience that got me to this new look, but it has made me a bit unforgettable.

Why Not Now? This Unique Look Makes Me Memorable.

Stage Time Day finally arrived. I stepped out of my breakout session early to join my nine peers for our opportunity to share for three minutes in front of a few thousand. When it was my turn, I had a small snafu, forgetting who was handing me the microphone. The bright lights distracted me from the routine we practiced. I stepped into the center of the stage to share my story and closed with, "Our adversities can uniquely qualify us to add value to others when we shift from self to serve."

As the crowd burst into a standing ovation, I walked to join my peers, who met me with hugs and high-fives. *God, we did it.* I was so focused on finishing well that I didn't contemplate the flood of people who would recognize me in the crowd during the final few days of the conference. I was incredibly blessed to be prayed for, hugged, and encouraged in the hallway. I met people I would have otherwise never known. It took bravery to show up on so many levels and just strive to shine through the scars and the unique me.

It's Time

By mid-August, it was time to visit my Miami team again. Ben took off from school to join me in the educational experience. Dr. Tse asked Ben great questions and had positive healing observations for me. His caring presence is always a blessing, and he reminded me to guard my right eye. "It's your only one, Diana."

As Ben and I walked over to the West Radiation Tower, it was like we were going back to visit family and friends. I often wondered how they remember me after all the patients they see every day.

Dr. Samuels introduced me to the term "phantom smells." I frequently thought I smelled something, and the boys would calmly say, "No, Mom. We don't smell anything."

On the drive back from Miami, Ben begrudgingly helped me prepare to lead my first DISC communication styles workshop with one eye. We were expecting about 100 people the next day, and I wanted to be ready for this new experience.

He survived listening to me, and the following day, I had the opportunity to tie my new blindspot into the blindspots we all have in communication. Transparency became key as I navigated a stage with one eye, unable to see what was coming on my left side.

For years, I avoided retaking my driver's license photo. But my address change and the number of years since my last photo triggered an in person visit. I scheduled an appointment online and filled out all the paperwork before I arrived. I hoped this would shorten the visit.

When it was my turn, the nice agent was not quite sure how to handle my look. She reviewed my paperwork and then looked at me.

"Is this permanent?" I'm sure she wondered if I had an eye under the flap.

"Yes, this is permanent."

"Then, we will need to take a vision test."

After a trip back to the car to get the glasses Bromley had "customized" to fit on my face—I had him cut the left lens off—I passed the vision test and left with a new driver's license with a mug shot that few can imitate.

As my healing progressed, I knew I needed to transition back to work. My heart felt conflicted. I missed the people, yet I didn't want to ignore the signs that my season there was coming to an end. I openly engaged with the ownership around my heart and desire to return part-time and then fade out of the business. I wasn't sure what was next, yet I knew that I didn't fit in the environment any longer.

James Clear said, "Every action you take is a vote for the type of person you want to be." This became a thought-provoking quote as I found myself recognized everywhere I went. My unique appearance made me memorable. It set the bar high for me to be a constant light.

While going through radiation, I attended a Beyond Success Values roundtable virtually. It was an incredible blessing to meet those who joined me for the seven weekly sessions. I knew it was time to put the facilitator training to work.

I started a Beyond Success roundtable at my house and extended the invitation to the women who had impacted my life in the last several years. Bromley and the boys kindly prepped our home each Sunday, creating a warm space for women of different aspects of my life to connect together.

In October, it was time to schedule MRI and PET scans again. I'm not sure I like these tests I really can't prepare for. All I can do is show up with confidence, pray for peace, hope I don't pass out during the IV part, and then wait patiently for the results. Every cancer patient can relate to this routine. These scans are our only safeguard because cancer can always come back once it has a foothold.

I could have seen the doctor to get my MRI results virtually; however, I really wanted to see Dr. Morcos before he relocated to Texas. He was the neurosurgeon who saved my life, so I had a strong desire to say goodbye in person and give him a gift.

Though I'd been traveling to Miami for almost a decade, I had never ventured to travel the Brightline before. I boarded the high speed rail and took in the scenery from West Palm Beach to Orlando and on to my destination. It felt odd to check into the hotel solo. Every other time, I'd been there with Bromley. I paused as I entered the room. Bromley had spent many nights alone here while I was in the hospital. What was it like to be him?

Dr. Morcos provided positive news on the MRI and PET scan and thanked me for bringing positivity to his team on my visits. As I headed back home, I contemplated ending "The Caring Bridge." *God, is the cancer journey over? Is it time to shift to a regular blog?*

Nine years before, when my cancer journey started, I journaled about writing and speaking and didn't take action. After my experience, I started to ignore the fear.

New Commitments

It didn't take long for the doors to open for speaking opportunities where I could share my story. Dear friends asked me to speak at a cancer fundraiser at Move Daytona. This was the first time I got to share my story in an unorthodox environment. Bromley and I arrived early to help set up for the Sunday yoga, CrossFit, and faith workout time. We also needed to figure out what part of the physical workout I could handle. After exercising, I donned the microphone headset and used the starfish image and taglines to share my story and encourage listeners. It was a far from flawless presentation, yet I was blessed when many came up to me afterward to share their stories.

This design was a reflection of my goal of how to live each day, even in the midst of pain, surgery, radiation, and healing. I'm far from perfect, and I just strive to get better every day and learn from yesterday.

- Starfish: Reflects one of my favorite stories with the little boy saving the starfish on the beach "It matters to that one."
- Light: Reminder to be a light in someone's day. The world needs a smile and someone who sees the possibilities.
- Make a Difference: A reminder to make a difference, even if small. Put away the excuses and look for a way to serve.
- One Matters: At times, I've hesitated to serve or volunteer because it wasn't "big enough." The starfish story has been an impactful reminder to me—one matters.
- Find Your Why: It's easy to "scroll" through life and not reflect on what makes you laugh, cry, and want to get up every morning. Find what makes you unique and share it.
- Positive Impact: My goal is to look for ways to make a positive impact on those I cross by. It may be a smile, it may be holding the door, it may be picking up the trash.
- Add Value & Value All: Find someone to add value to each day, and don't forget that all of God's creations matter.

After my first speaking opportunity, it was time to prepare to host the first Live2Lead in the Daytona area. This transition from the narrow life focus of radiation and healing to returning to work, speaking, and hosting an event was stretching me in new ways as I strived to honor my commitments.

One of those commitments was to Greyson. He joked with me in the hospital that I looked like I was ready for Halloween Horror Nights. Well, I committed to attending with Greyson and his friend even though the surgical area had healed considerably, and I no longer fit in as a scare actor. Navigating through dark houses reminded me I had weaknesses. I needed help getting around in dark spaces with one eye. Greyson and his friend were quick to help navigate me through the houses and ensure I didn't falter with my monovision.

As I prepared to share at my home church, I found a few more challenges. It's often easier to talk to strangers than a group of people who know you and have been praying for you and cheering you on. The building was much wider, and learning to navigate and engage the full crowd with a narrowed vision always offers an opportunity for growth.

Pastor Michael kicked off the time with an interview, probing with a few questions that connected to my story. Fifteen years before, I would never have walked onto that stage or shared to that level. As I closed the talk, I mentioned that when I lead business presentations or workshops, I ask each person to share their takeaway. I was tempted to shake up the church environment and challenge this group to share, but I opted to close out and hand the stage back to the worship team. It was touching to interact with the church family after the service on the impact and the questions. I felt awe as they declared me a warrior and the toughest person they knew. Some even asked, "How do you do that with a smile?" Their encouragement helped me raise my bar.

The next event would be the area's first Live2Lead event hosted at White Chapel. I wanted to set a goal of fifty in attendance but fought that need for a number and reminded myself that my value is to be satisfied to impact one. I have a decal that says Impact One. It's easy to get distracted and forget that one matters.

The event was scheduled to include a video rebroadcast and two local speakers. Since Veterans Day was close, I invited one of my favorite veterans, Dr. Hal Kusher, to share his view on leadership. He agreed to come even though he was limiting his speaking events. I had the honor to introduce him as a medical angel that greatly impacted my life. As he accepted the microphone, he kindly shifted the compliments to me, recognizing my positive leadership and spirit to fight.

Many days, I don't understand all the whys of this cancer journey, but I do know I have been incredibly blessed with meeting people that I would never have encountered. You see, the journey isn't about cancer.

Maintaining Routine

I admit I find comfort in the routines of life, especially when they let me spend time with the boys. So, it felt good to head out for our fourth Family Camp in Rome, Georgia. Familiar faces and new friends greeted us when we arrived. I couldn't help but reflect on my sons' growth over the past year as I watched the boys engage with girls their age. Even with one eye, I proved to be a cornhole force. It was fun to laugh and try new sports with one eye.

The week before Thanksgiving, I was blessed to be interviewed on a global radio show, "The Leader's Edge." Steve and Ernie hosted multiple prep sessions, and I thought I was scripted pretty well. Then, they asked a few off-script questions. If the audience could have seen my face, they would have sensed the pair caught me a bit off-guard. Fortunately, only the hosts could see my face; I sounded poised and ready to the radio audience. It was easier to engage in the small crowd and over Zoom.

We headed to my parents for Thanksgiving and an opportunity to share at the church of my youth. My mom set everything up for the Sunday after Thanksgiving when the family would be in town. Taking the stage of that familiar place I had not been to in years brought a flood of memories. I had taken part in a musical called *Down by the Creek Bank* as a child.

Familiar faces dotted the crowd. One of my keys to overcoming my fear of public speaking is to make the talking points about the crowd and consider how it can impact their lives. This opportunity looks very different from others, with my parents, siblings, nieces, nephews, relatives, and former teachers in the crowd. I felt blessed to hear the stories and emotions my message sparked.

Despite the positive feedback when I shared my story, doubt and fear sank in when I thought about writing a book. What makes me worthy? Amazingly, though, when doubts sink in, God places people in our path to remind us that others need to hear the story. People need motivation to move forward. This quote by Morgan Snyder in *Becoming a King* was a reminder for me to trust the slow, steady process and the learnings along the path: "But what if the desire was planted in us first and foremost to feel the slow and steady process of becoming the kind of person who can handle all that has been entrusted to him by God."

As we closed 2024, the firsts with one eye kept piling up. Laughter and humility became friends on the journey. The Ormond Beach parade had been an annual routine, and it felt pretty simple when I had two eyes. Navigating all those people and their stares was a bit much on a chilly Florida evening post-surgery. I was incredibly thankful for a hand to guide me through the crowds and the people. Sometimes, we need a dear friend or spouse to help us see what we don't see.

Many think saying goodbye to an eye may be the hardest thing I did all year, yet, I am torn. Yes, it was hard, but the benefits outweighed the difficulty. I had to choose between living longer and keeping an eye, my physical appearance, or staying with my boys. Saying goodbye to my dream property may have been harder. We signed the final contract at a price lower than my heart thought it was worth. I walked around the house with tears, pondering the many memories with the boys and Bromley—from first experiences, hurricane bonding, water slide parties, and laughter to watching my boys grow and mature.

It may have been a harder goodbye because the underlying cause was not just the housing market; it was also tied to people not honoring their word in a tough season of my life. I kept trying to figure out how to hang on when all the doors were closing. I worked (and it was work) to express gratitude for our time there and accept our shift in location. It was hard to say goodbye to the place that held all those memories and housed that season of my boys' lives.

Reflection

We don't have many weather seasons in Florida. Yet, mentally, I navigated through more seasons than we experienced in Pennsylvania. The transition from a radiation routine back into a home routine was a new challenge. The finality of the season of having two eyes was reinforced when the driver's license clerk asked, "Is this permanent?"

The greater challenge was to start to share my story with transparency and humility. For many years, I did not act on my desire to write a book and share my story. Focusing on making an impact on just one helped me prepare with an emphasis on the audience. It couldn't be about me. Many times, people share their stories because they want to get it all out. Sharing with the desire to impact one and influence the audience positively makes all the difference.

- What items in your life are you putting off? If you went through old journals, what would you find?
- This quote was impactful to me: "Every action you take is a vote for the type of person you want to be." What does it evoke in you?
- "Is this permanent" elicited some unexpected internal reflection for me. Yes, the skin flap over my left eye socket is permanent. Yet, I still get to choose my response and whether or not the limitations of one eye or my new look are permanent. What does "Is this permanent" evoke in you?

Application

- Write down five "dreams" you have been putting off.
- Take thirty minutes of quiet time to reflect on why it's a dream and why you've been procrastinating and to identify the next steps.
- Where are you letting a "new permanent" impact your positive mindset and limit your response and freedom to choose? What mindset shifts do you need to make?
- Take a minute to ponder the season of life you are in. If you struggle to find yourself and your purpose in this season, set aside thirty minutes to listen to quiet music and reflect. Jot down what comes to mind, let tears flow, and connect with how your adversity and your season can add value to another.

CHAPTER NINETEEN

What Is Normal?

As I considered how I would find the time to write this book, God subtly reminded me that for a cancer patient, just like every person on the earth, our journey here doesn't end until death. We walk through seasons, but each one shifts to the next. We look for normal, but every trial, every new job, every new season brings a new normal. Honestly, what is normal? In my case, normal has become watching for new infections and pains and showing up for every follow-up appointment to check in and ensure progress.

Nearly a year after my surgery, I started struggling with sinus blockage. I did a Google search to find a natural remedy and found a suggestion for warm compresses. I'm not sure what I did wrong because that led to some loss of skin and seeping, almost like a sunburn on the skin flap over my eye.

God had it all timed out. On the day my eye flap looked miserable, I had a doctor's appointment already scheduled. He confirmed my eye flap was fine and swabbed my nose for an infection. Three days later, the office called to tell me I had a staph infection and needed oral antibiotics.

Meanwhile, the area under the flap near my cheekbone had become very inflamed. I reached out to Dr. Kushner and Dr. Tse. Both suggested I go to the ER. I wasn't surprised by the recommendation, yet I cringed at the thought of walking into an ER with my look. How long would it take to tell the story of one eye and get to the point of the visit? Thankfully, Dr. Kushner called ahead, so the doctors there were ready for me. At the hospital, they ushered me to a room and immediately started strong IV antibiotics.

Dr. Kushner came to visit me the next day. He had discussed my case with the ER doctor and promised to stay close to my case. During the three nights I spent in the ER observation area, the team took good care of me, and Dr. Kushner checked on me more often than most people in his position.

Diana with Dr. Hal Kushner at their favorite lunch spot.

What Is Normal?

There were no showers, only hallway bathrooms, in this section. It took me back to my cabin days as I stood in the bathroom taking a sponge bath. I smiled as I reminded the nurses I had no sense of smell, so I had to rely on them to tell me if the sponge bath wasn't taking effect.

As usual, my low heart rate and blood pressure triggered extra attention and watchful eyes. I often felt a tap on my shoulder from the nurse in the middle of the night to make sure I was okay. Between IV treatments, I was blessed to be able to put in about 7,000 steps that first day.

The next day, I walked by a dear gal with a mental disorder. She stepped out of her room to loudly question, "What the hell happened to you?" The nurse came quickly to put her back in her room. She stated loudly, "I've never seen shit like that. What happened to her?" Normally, I stayed to talk to those with questions, yet I knew she was not in the right state to handle a conversation. For the rest of my lap, I moved away from her room and offered a prayer for her. I have to admit the question and her statement of never seeing anything quite like me prompted some internal laughter.

I hoped day three would be my last at the hospital. But until I was discharged, I was determined to look for ways to brighten the days of the people around me. A grumpy, disrespectful CNA caught my attention at one point. The nurse she served with remained poised and calm despite being chastised by the CNA in my room.

An hour later, when I walked down the hall to get more coffee, the grumpy CNA started to scold me for drinking too much coffee. The patient nurse stepped in and offered to help, prompting the CNA to go find my beverage. As we waited, I complimented the sweet nurse for her poise and patience. She thanked me for noticing and proceeded to tell me how beautiful I was. She said she had been watching me walk the halls with a calm smile and sweet aura. Considering the puffy and injured eye flap and hair that hadn't been washed in three days, I felt good she noticed my inner beauty.

Once again, I recognized my hospital visit had a bigger purpose than my healing. When I'm postured to serve, I am uniquely imperfect—something easily noticed—and uniquely qualified to connect and bring hope.

Reflection

My unique cancer journey means I have to redefine my normal. At the same time, my outward appearance—the part others see at first glance—constantly reminds me I am unique—uniquely imperfect but uniquely qualified.

Ten to fifteen years ago, I took my "normal" for granted. I had two eyes and good health. Small adversities often distracted me. I recall cringing at the thought of messing up my weekend plans by going to the Emergency Room on a Friday night.

Today, I have a different view of normal as well as a reformed appreciation of a weekend spent in the Emergency Room. I've learned to accept the kindness of others and make the most of my time with a new audience of medical staff.

- I don't love emergency rooms, but I do love the people I have met and the opportunity to bring light to their often "thankless world." When we move away from our pain to encourage others, our pain lightens.
- Know your audience. It's not always the right time to tell your story. In the ER, a woman with obvious mental problems saw my face and began to rant about the oddity. She wanted an explanation. And

while, normally, I'm happy to oblige, in that moment, it wouldn't have helped her. Sometimes, we need to walk on.

- Beauty is not external; true beauty radiates from within.
    - I have strived to be "unmasked" for about ten years now. This is who I am. Somehow, most people quickly move past the external and see the sparkle in my remaining eye combined with the smile I try to keep on my face. They recognize the light and warmth I have inside. Our imperfections can uniquely qualify us to lift others up. When we are authentic and okay with our imperfections, we can become an inspiration to others.

Applications

- What would your life be like especially the ladies, if you took off the makeup or the mask for a day and allowed yourself to be you? Or perhaps you need to drop the facade and let a tear or two roll down your face.
- Where are you waiting for "normal" or "ideal" and need to just move forward?
    -
    -
- What adversities are you navigating that uniquely qualify you to extend hope and encouragement to

others? List them along with the lessons you have been learning on the journey.

-
-
-
-

CHAPTER TWENTY

The Journey Continues

Well, I hoped the March ER visit was the end of my cancer season. I knew I would have follow-ups, but I was ready to be done. The UM team checked my MRIs and determined the redness on the flap coming and going was a mystery. Since I continued to feel healthy and strong, we moved forward until the next set of images in June.

Giving Back to Those Who Cared for Me

The Patient Advisory Council at UM asked me to speak to the Nursing Leaders on April 6, 2024. I quickly said yes. I am always honored to share my story and thank those who served me. Plus, this event would be on the anniversary of my surgery.

The boys traveled with me to experience the train as well as fit in some museum time after my medical appointments. I also took them to one of my favorite Miami restaurants to celebrate one year post-surgery. As I finalized my preparation on Saturday morning, I asked the hotel clerk to print my notes. He handed it to me with a note on top, "You are an inspiration."

At the event, I sat with nursing leaders I had never met. It was an honor to hear their stories. When the time came for the patient guests to share, I joined five others on stage. I had prepped and completed several dry runs, yet standing in front of a crowd who had served and cared for people like me evoked great emotion.

I always get a bit teary when I share my cancer story, yet this crowd watched me choke back tears, stop, and regain my composure before going on many times. I felt honored to step out of my routine to give back to the nursing leadership team.

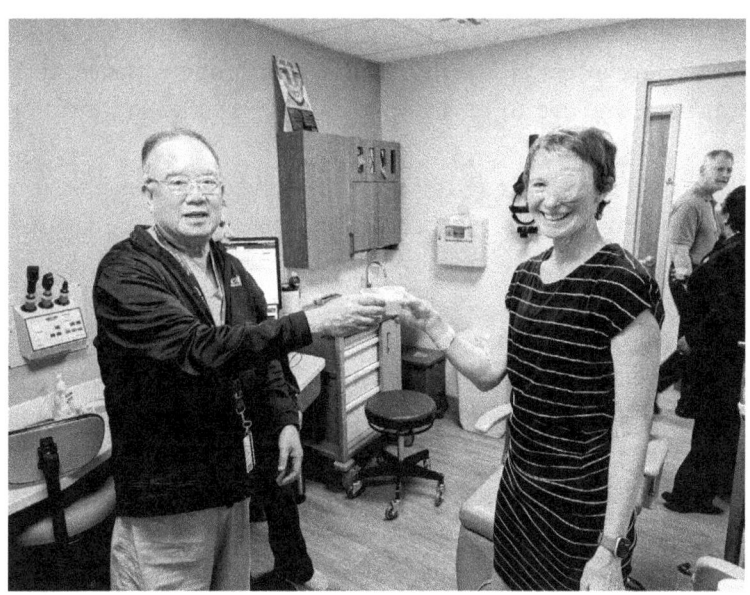

10-year toast as a patient and cancer thriver.

Giving Back to Those Who Stood with Me

Though I was anxious to return to as normal a life as possible, it was important to me to work from home more than usual to be near Greyson and Ben and my family. True to my nature to please everyone, I struggled at times with that focus and commitment.

We continued to serve at White Chapel as well. One Sunday, as I stood in the lobby talking and greeting, I saw a new elementary student walk in the door with his grandfather. When he saw me, we locked eyes, and he bolted across the lobby to me. I knelt down so I could better engage with him.

"You only have one eye," the youngster said.

"Hi," I replied. "What's your name?"

"Johnny."

"You're right, Johnny, I only have one eye. But I'm thankful to have one eye. I tell you what, every time you see me, I want my one eye to be a reminder to you to be grateful for your two eyes."

This became a routine every Sunday. Our conversation would vary at times. And some days, he thought he needed to try it out by covering one eye and walking around. My unique look opened the door of communication for me and a young, troubled boy.

One dear older lady also inquired about my eye each Sunday. After two weeks of explaining I had no eye under the skin flap and it wouldn't improve, I moved on to a smile and an assurance that I was healing. She had good intentions but had problems listening and processing the information.

Not So Routine

At the end of June, I headed to Twin Lakes for my routine MRI and PET scan. I was thankful I had found an insurance company that understands your illness, doctors, and needs. At the beginning of my cancer life, it sometimes felt like a part-time job to fight for benefits, approvals, referrals, and more. I can't imagine what it's like for the retired generation to navigate the systems and the red tape.

Modern technology is a blessing and, at times, a potential source of anxiety. About thirty minutes after the scans, I could access and review the written report. I didn't understand all the medical jargon, yet I could sense the news was not all good. I paused and shared my reports through the UM app; this news was beyond my control and understanding.

After I shared the report and images with my doctors, the Miami medical team called. They saw indications of tumor growth behind my right eye and in the skin flap area. Dr. Benjamin reviewed her recommendation with me prior to the final determination from the tumor board. Although surgery could remove the tumor so they could send it for evaluation, she strongly recommended the Gamma Knife procedure in radiology. This would be safer for me and less intense for healing.

Dr. Benjamin told me not to worry and just wait for the tumor board review. They would provide me with the best recommendation. My family had an Alaskan cruise scheduled for the end of July to celebrate a normal summer and three milestone birthdays. Greyson, Ben, and I would be sixteen, thirteen, and fifty, respectively. She responded with confidence, "Diana, we will do the procedure before you go. Don't cancel that vacation."

Soon, we had a date. We locked in July 18 for the Gamma Knife procedure. During the seven weeks of radiation, I walked by the Gamma Knife sign every day and wondered what it was. Well, it was time for me to experience what it was.

As we waited, Bromley and I focused on our early July vacation and time with the extended family. We had missed that during 2023 due to my radiation, but this year, they were bringing the party to Florida thanks to my niece. We would host dinners and plan fun activities.

Many times along the way, I nearly forgot my true role. I didn't want to be a cancer patient who just showed up for appointments. I wanted to be a light, a ray of hope. Even as I navigated insurance and approvals, I needed to be a positive guide for my family. The little time to focus on me has proven to be an incredible protection from hiding in a ball to escape the chaos.

Bromley and I researched the Gamma Knife procedure. We found information consistent with what the doctors had told us. It would be a same-day procedure, and I would have a helmet attached to keep me still. I might have side effects popping up a few months after. There were more than a few unknowns going into the procedure. Still, it sounded simpler than my last surgery.

On the day of the procedure, we rose early and walked from the hotel to UHealth West. It felt like coming back home as we retraced the path we took for my radiation treatments. True to Bromley's nature, we arrived early and sat in the waiting room, talking about what was different since my last visit.

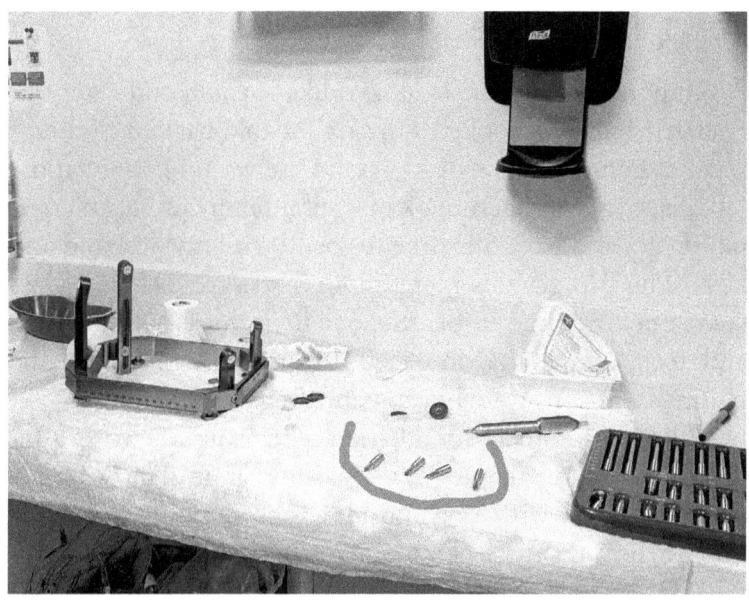

Prior to the procedure, the doctors wanted an MRI. But first, the nurses started my IV and kindly gave me the relaxation and nausea medication I asked for. Before the drugs took effect, they explained they would be putting four screw-like pins up against my forehead to hold the helmet on, and then they fitted me with the large contraption.

I recall being carted over to the MRI and napping on and off throughout the scan; however, I have no recollection of the Gamma Room. I don't even remember getting dressed following the procedure.

As promised, I was back to work the next day and able to think well and focus. The challenge came when I tried to sleep. I had two sore spots on the front of my head and two on the back from the pins of the helmet. Those things didn't matter, though. I was just happy to be home.

Alaska, Here We Come

A temporary airline crisis looked like it could endanger our Alaska trip. So, I booked fully refundable backup flights. I was not going to let anything get in the way of this vacation.

The trip could be a book in itself. I felt incredibly blessed to hit fifty and have this time to spend with my husband and boys. The trip gave us many more firsts. We had first-class seats, our first time in Seattle, our first cruise with a tween and teen, and many one-eyed navigation firsts. Plus, the nature excursions were beyond amazing.

The boys quickly found friends to hang out with after dinner or during the at-sea days. Our family's favorite day was in Skagway with early morning rock climbing and afternoon helicopter flight. Ever since I started to navigate with one eye, my rock climbing usually consisted of making a sincere effort and stepping away after making it part way up. This time, I was determined to make it to the top. I took breaks and used my elbows—which isn't normal. I was committed to finishing. Like life battles, it takes commitment to get to the finish line, especially if it's hard.

After rock climbing, we scheduled a helicopter tour to a sled dog area. However, fog grounded it. The upgrade was another helicopter ride with a former Army pilot who landed on a glacier. What a magnificent gift. The four of us walked alone on the huge piece of ice and admired the beauty.

We spent most of my fiftieth birthday at sea, and I took the time to write to Dr. Tse and Dr. Kushner to thank them for the key role they played in getting me to this birthday.

I know many people dread the thought of turning fifty. However, I look at each celebration as a sign of victory; I'm still in the game.

Gamma Evaluation

In September, I had another MRI to evaluate the success of the Gamma Knife. Once again, I felt like I was preparing for a test without any way to study. Instead, I vowed to continue the fight for my health, both physical and spiritual, and show up with confidence.

The morning of the MRI, I wrote notes to each of the techs that would help me that day. I wanted them to know I appreciate their service and care even though their days must be a weary mix of good news and tough news throughout the day.

A DISC workshop awaited me as soon as I finished the MRI. I'm always honored to facilitate DISC communication workshops. The training has greatly impacted my professional and personal life.

This particular workshop was for a company that provides solutions for the medical industry. I related to the importance of their "why" more than most. My portion of the training began with the story of my literal blind spot to introduce the concept of the communication blind spots everyone faces.

After the workshop, I stopped by the imaging site for the CD of my results. Usually, I can skim the reports and tell if it is good news or not, but this time the medical jargon had me more confused than normal.

The next morning, I took my quiet time on the beach and then sent emails to my Miami medical team. I thanked them for fighting with me and noted my MRI data was uploaded, and I was committed to fighting. My neurosurgeon called that night. She told me she appreciated my email, sunrise photos, and a positive mindset. Plus, I remind her of her sister, who is battling cancer.

Most importantly, she told me there was definitely good news in the MRI. Some areas that appeared to have normal cells had grown from July to September. The growth was minor and needed to be reviewed by the tumor board. She would update me on Friday.

The next day, I met with the radiologist, who noted the similar good news. The areas treated with the Gamma Knife looked clear. There were solid indications that the tumor had responded to the targeted radiation. Thank God! The radiologist also shared his view on other areas that needed attention and proactively scheduled the Gamma Knife, so I had a spot on the calendar.

Dr. Benjamin and the tumor board confirmed that we needed to eliminate the spots quickly. I asked her if she thought the tumor looked like it could spread to areas the Gamma Knife couldn't treat. She agreed our approach was more spot welding and suggested we bring Dr. Feun, my oncologist, back in to prevent the tumor from growing to areas outside the scope of the Gamma Knife.

The following week, I met with Dr. Fuen. He agreed to do additional studies. He would send my tumor from April 2023 to Caris Life Sciences to get more detailed results. We would reconvene in thirty days.

Priorities

The longer I walked this path, the more I weighed my life priorities. After talking with Dr. Feun, I cringed at leaving for four days to meet with an unappreciative client who was not communicating. I went to honor my word; however, this visit made me reevaluate these kinds of trips.

When I returned, a flood of emotions hit me. None of us know what day is our last. Every single person needs to make the best of each day, yet my situation felt a little more pressing. I felt like I was juggling work and home. And the upcoming homecoming dance seemed to be competing with my anniversary weekend. Every decision had become emotional and reflective.

Over dinner at the Rose Villa, Bromley and I talked about the logistics of our anniversary weekend. He had a colonoscopy slated for our October 7 anniversary. I couldn't help but think that would be a good excuse for us to stay home. He would need to prep on Sunday. That wouldn't be fun if we were away. But when I mentioned that to him, he said he thought we could still go away.

"Okay, Diana, give in to your humanness."

Trying to remain composed, I said, "Greyson's homecoming is Saturday."

Bromley immediately knew what I was thinking. "It's his first one, and I don't know how many I will be around for."

"You definitely need to be here for that."

After a brief pause for tears, my peacemaker nature attempted to "fix" the fact we were missing our anniversary getaway. My husband calmly reminded me I didn't need to push myself. We would go away another time.

My mom blessed us by coming to visit for a few weeks during my next Gamma Knife procedure. As I prepped for

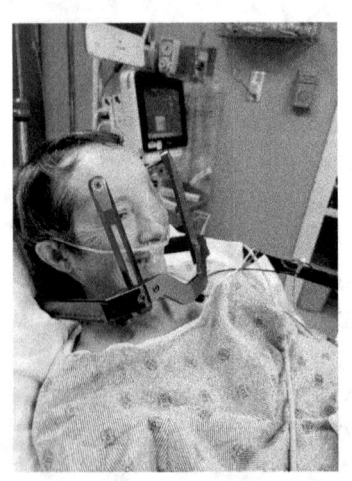

our departure, mixed messages came in from my insurance. I called Miami and the insurance companies to make sure everything was approved in time. With today's technology, the chaos and silo mentality of the insurance industry amazes me. But before we left, everything was cleared.

As the nurse checked me in, I asked him if they knew of a way to avoid the sore spots on my head. That was my greatest concern. He smiled understandingly but didn't have any good suggestions. The neurosurgery fellow came to numb my head as the nurse gave me relaxing meds, and we repeated the process I'd gone through just a few months before.

The pins didn't seem to be as painful as we waited for the MRI, and the special cocktail they gave me for relaxation and nausea wasn't as draining as the last time. I stayed awake for the transfer to the Gamma Knife room.

Dr Kubicek explained this procedure would be shorter than the last time, and once again, I would not be able to move my head with the frame. Between the boredom and the drugs, I ended up falling asleep; however, at one point, I awoke with a jerk. I dreamt I had overslept and missed the appointment. With my hand in the air, I opened my eyes and felt the headlock in place. I wasn't going anywhere; however, for a few minutes, I was afraid I had messed up the image by moving.

After the procedure, the team came in and assured me my head hadn't moved. All had gone well, and another MRI in two months would tell us what we needed to know.

I felt much better this time than the last and felt confident Bromley and I could walk to Panera to eat. The nurse thought otherwise. She wanted me to give the meds a little more time to wear off and suggested the hospital cafeteria so I could stay in the wheelchair. I guess God just wanted to demonstrate His perfect timing again.

The night before, at our hotel check-in, a kind lady with a troubled face had approached me. She recognized me from a Maxwell conference. She had discussed her husband's medical condition with me at the conference. I remembered her face, but her name escaped me. I thought it was Nora.

I woke the morning of my procedure, praying for a way to run into her again. I regretted not getting her information so I could stay in touch with her. As Bromley wheeled me into the cafeteria, there she was. We joined her for lunch, and she shared her contact information with me. (Her name was not Nora). What a blessed reminder that God is always with us.

After lunch, I held Bromley's hand and walked—against medical advice—to Bascom Palmer to see Dr. Tse. We reviewed my progress, and Dr. Tse shared some of my past stories with his fellow. Then, Denise, his nurse, came in to give me a hug. She said, "I always enjoy seeing you. You always bring light and a positive smile with you."

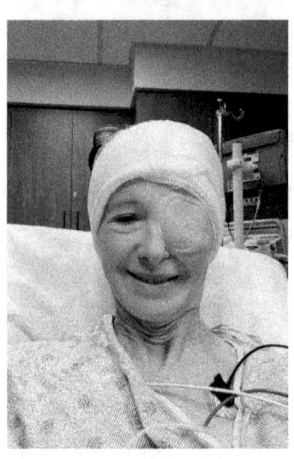

Bromley and I arrived at the Brightline train station early. I am certain the Miami vibe was jealous of my gauze headband. Within an hour, we boarded and headed home. My energy level was higher during this routine, so I used the time to write and read. We pulled into our driveway at about 10:30. Just in time to give the boys hugs and talk about their days before we all went to bed.

The four screw areas didn't seem as sore as the last go-round. But when I woke up the next morning, I felt a bit groggy. I wasn't sure if it was tied to the Gamma Knife, the light anesthesia, or my allergies. I considered it a pleasure to make breakfast for the boys and pack their lunches as they got ready for school.

I navigated work meetings via Zoom and made time for naps throughout the day. About four in the afternoon, I decided I could navigate outside. I had a hard-to-describe tightness near the skin flap. It wasn't sore, but I felt constricted as I moved from the car to the grocery store. That night, I had a little discomfort, but Bromley and the boys said the flap looked normal. By seven, I was ready for bed, which was quite early for me. True to my routine, I stopped to talk with each of the boys and give them a hug goodnight. Our family was focusing on a Fruit of the Spirit each week, and I reminded them the word for this week was Patience.

Within a few days, I felt more like myself and ready to resume the routine. As some of you reading can relate, healing from a procedure is very different from healing from the emotion around the procedure or healing in a generation. My head soreness could be gone in a few weeks, but that does not mean the cancer is gone. A month later, bald spots appeared on my head. My husband was afraid to tell me; I just laughed—let's add a bald spot to my unique look.

Reflection

As the MRI started to show spot issues even past the intense surgery, I felt a pull to be more aware of each moment.

The Second Gamma Knife procedure became a mental struggle for me. I had a hard time scheduling anything past that date. It just felt too unknown, too disappointing, and I didn't want to do the head screws again.

It is hard to explain what the left side of my face feels like. "Different from the right" doesn't do it justice. I feel like our emotional or mental battles are much like that; on the outside, all looks well, providing a mask for the real sensations.

- Where do you feel uneasiness on your journey? You may not be able to explain why it doesn't feel right.
- What are you navigating that is hard to explain? Maybe you feel alone because you think others can't relate to the journey.

Application

This application time requires a mix of reflection and journaling. I recommend breaking the questions out over a few days.

- What mask are you hiding behind? Your demeanor, your makeup, and your look may be masking your true feelings. Where do you need to acknowledge your humanness?

    -
    -
    -
    -
    - Gals: Did you take the challenge to go one day without makeup? If not, do that now. Then, reflect the next day on what emotion that evoked. Was it hard to be authentically you?

- Repeating a procedure multiple times can be defeating. My talk track was brave, yet inside, I felt some doubt and disappointment. Where is your disappointment? If you feel stuck in those disappointments, consider a life coach or counselor.

    -
    -
    -
    -

Uniquely Imperfect, Uniquely Qualified

- I feel the pressure to live more intentionally as the scans show different issues. I realize not everyone reading this has cancer; however, I am frequently reminded of the life insurance lesson I shared earlier. "Someone isn't coming home tonight; we just don't know who it is." We all need to live with greater intention. Where do you need to be more intentional? Your days are no more guaranteed than those of a stage five cancer patient. Don't wait until you have a diagnosis to practice being intentional.

    o
    o
    o
    o

Afterword

I realize not everyone can relate to a cancer journey. Perhaps someone gave you this book, and you wonder how it's relevant to you. But my story is a testimony bigger than my cancer. It's truly the tale of one uniquely imperfect person who found that as I shifted away from a focus on why me, I was blessed with some touching moments to serve and be a light. I discovered what it means to be Uniquely Imperfect, Uniquely Qualified.

I can say with confidence my journey isn't over. My faith tells me I'm not home yet. I fervently pray that regardless of how many days I have left on this earth, my legacy of choosing to focus on the positive and embracing my imperfections and adversities will add value to others and spark them to move their attention from their scars to their shine.

As I went through old journals to bring you this story, I thought about the array of people who the book might impact. I want to encourage fellow cancer patient who needs a story to relate to, as well as the family members of cancer patients who don't understand the pain. I also hope my story helps those who suffer from non-medical cancers that steal their joy.

And to my dear boys, who I pray saw a mom who was willing to fight for them and choose positivity and my dear family and friends who fought with me, I want you to know how I feel blessed to be here. I am blessed to know you, and I thank you for being with me through this spot in my story.

Afterword

I know that sometimes life sucks. Too often, bad stuff happens to good people. Yes, sometimes the medical system is a mess, and sometimes, life is so full of unknowns that you want to run and hide.

If any of those statements resonate, I have a challenge for you. Don't go there. Fight. My journals reminded me of this quote, which became so real to me in 2014.

WHAT CANCER CAN NOT DO

Cancer is so limited …
It cannot cripple love,
It cannot shatter hope,
It cannot corrode faith,
It cannot destroy peace,
It cannot kill friendship,
It cannot suppress memories,
It cannot silence courage,
It cannot invade the soul,
It cannot steal eternal life,
It cannot conquer the spirit.[2]
– Author Unknown

You get to choose.

- I choose to laugh when people stare at me.
- I chose to smile and bring hope and grace to my medical team.

---

[2] You can download a version of this poem here: https://mycancerresources.com/what-cancer-cannot-do-poem-printable/

- I chose to laugh at my blind spots.
    - I can't smell the icky stuff.
    - I run into things or people that are in my blind spot.
    - I cringe at driving in tight spaces and parking garages.
    - I am entertained when children throwing tantrums look up at me and freeze—they put everything into perspective without saying a word.
    - I enjoy the conversations that come when kids look at me and ask the same question every week. What happens to your eye? Where is your eye?
- Don't lose the battle of your mind and your mindset. That is the superpower that God has given you.
- People may not remember the jobs you had, the places you served, or how old you were, but they will remember how you showed up and whether you were a light in the dark or brought dark to the light.
- Be the light. Be the smile.
- Our adversities can uniquely qualify us to add value to others when we can shift from self to serve. It's not about me and my imperfections.
- I am Uniquely Imperfect, which Uniquely Qualifies me to add value to others when I shift from a focus on poor me to how I can use this adversity and my story to add value to others.
- Show up well every day.

I'd like to invite you to visit my blog.

Acknowledgments

In 2014, as I started this cancer journey, I journaled about writing a book someday. Ten years later, the inaugural Book in a Weekend opportunity sparked my interest. Thanks to Tim Elmore and Sangram Vajre for providing the forum to prepare first-time authors and challenge us to move forward to write the book.

Acknowledgments

Thanks to Mark Cole and his inspiring feedback as a "Book Shark" with the Book in a Weekend team. His feedback was so valuable and challenged me to keep moving forward.

Many medical professionals are mentioned in this book. Dr. Hal Kushner and Dr. David Tse are two medical inspirations on my journey. Without cancer, I would never have met these two wonderful leaders within the medical field. They bless my life in so many ways.

My husband and two boys who walked with me on this journey and helped make space for me to research and write.

To the many faithful friends at my church who encouraged me every Sunday and, without knowing it, kept dropping hints to write a book and share my story. Many times when I doubted that I was worthy to write a book, you would bless me with a comment or a note recommending I do.

Special thanks to my dear friend Misty for the family photos and to my niece Rowan Eshbach for her creative addition to the cover design.

I am worthy because I am a child of the King. He loves me and has guided me through this journey.

One Eye, One Life, One Matters.

You matter, and thank you for inspiring me to Keep Smiling!

About the Author

*Our stories and our example make us credible
and able to connect
with our team and our audience.
Our adversities can be a great opportunity
to extend a hand and add value to others.*

Resilient, transparent, and positive. These words accurately and succinctly describe Diana Fritz's characteristics as an executive leader, cancer survivor, board member, wife, mother, and committed volunteer.

About the Author

Throughout her extensive career spanning more than twenty-five years, Diana has consistently sought and embraced opportunities for leadership, teamwork, and personal growth. Her professional journey has provided her with progressively responsible leadership roles in executive leadership, operations, administration, organizational health, human resources, business planning, and technology. This diverse and well-rounded career enables Diana to connect effectively with any audience, and her transparent approach to sharing her medical experiences fosters a sense of relatability and motivation among individuals in the healthcare and medical fields.

Since her cancer diagnosis in 2014, Diana has embraced the concept of being a "cancer thriver" and endeavors to be a source of light within the walls of hospitals, doctors' offices, and wherever her path leads her. During the pandemic, she had the unique opportunity to serve in a capacity that involved providing leadership and guidance related to COVID-19 testing and vaccine sites, stepping in, and fulfilling critical roles during a period when leadership was lacking.

Diana Fritz is a member of the Maxwell Leadership Executive Team, Corporate Facilitator, and DISC Consultant. More importantly, she is a proud and humble mother of two teen boys, Greyson and Benjamin, and the wife of Bromley.

As an author and keynote speaker, Diana appreciates the opportunity to connect, share, and inspire with messages around overcoming adversity, choosing a positive mindset, and leading with a servant's heart. Her personal mission is to provide value, make a positive impact, and treat every individual as a valued client.

One Eye, One Life, One Matters.
Connect with Diana at GRITUIUQ.com

CONNECT WITH DIANA

Connect with me.
I'd be honored to encourage
you on your journey.

GRITUIUQ.com

OUR ADVERSITIES CAN UNIQUELY QUALIFY US.... FOCUS ON THE POSITIVE

Power of Positive Mindset • Overcoming Communication Blind Spots • Breaking Down Silos - Teamwork • Leading Through Adversity & Crisis

KEYNOTE SPEAKER: DIANA FRITZ

GRITUIUQ.com

"A GOOD COACH CAN CHANGE A GAME. A GREAT COACH CAN CHANGE A LIFE."
-JOHN WOODEN-

DO YOU HAVE A DESIRE TO GROW YOURSELF OR YOUR BUSINESS TO THE NEXT LEVEL?

DO YOU WISH SOME DAYS YOU HAD A COACH, SOMEONE TO PUSH YOU AND HOLD YOU ACCOUNTABLE?

ARE YOU FEELING "STUCK" WITH A RECENT DIAGNOSIS?

SIGN UP FOR A 15-MINUTE COMPLIMENTARY COACHING CALL TO DETERMINE IF THIS WOULD BE A WIN-WIN PARTNERSHIP.

GRITUIUQ.com

OVERCOMING COMMUNICATION BLIND SPOTS WORKSHOP

- Discover your personal communication style.

- Learn about other communication styles and how best to connect.

- Identify where your blind spots may be creating conflict or hindering growth.

- Learn the importance of a balanced team/family and communication styles.

- Identify actionable steps to improve your connection with others.

The MAXWELL DISC METHOD

GRITUIUQ.com

THIS BOOK IS PROTECTED INTELLECTUAL PROPERTY

The author of this book values Intellectual Property and has utilized Instant IP, a groundbreaking technology. Instant IP is the patented, blockchain-based solution for Intellectual Property protection.

Blockchain is a distributed public digital record that can not be edited. Instant IP timestamps the author's ideas, creating a smart contract, thus an immutable digital asset that proves ownership and establishes a first to use / first to file event.

Protected by Instant IP ™

LEARN MORE AT INSTANTIP.TODAY

www.ingramcontent.com/pod-product-compliance
Lightning Source LLC
Chambersburg PA
CBHW052136070526
44585CB00017B/1852